"Economics and its applications are considered to be a combination of arts and science. When it comes to engineering economics, a mathematical model is more intuitive to create a unique bridge between abstract science and predictive future. Life Cycle Cost Analysis is a framework that is fundamentally based on a mathematical model whose importance is far-reaching and ever-increasing. In this context, Nirjhar Chakravorti's book is highly relevant. Nirjhar has unfolded the mystery of Life Cycle Cost Analysis with a lucid and step-by-step explanation which can be useful for anyone interested in engineering economics. The Life Cycle Cost Analysis methodology adopted by Nirjhar is unique.

"The Life Cycle Cost Analysis framework explained in this book is a highly rigorous architectural plan that has been extremely beneficial to me, my students, and my clients. This framework has been most useful to our company, Halloran Associates. We integrated this framework into our company's Life Cycle Cost Analysis Model. I am extremely delighted that Nirjhar has explained this framework in his book which can be useful for experts as well as the students who are willing to learn about Life Cycle Cost Analysis. Nirjhar has explored the issues related to Life Cycle Cost Analysis in depth and it will be so helpful in the complex analysis. This is an amazing book for someone interested in Life Cycle Cost Analysis."

Dr. David G. Halloran, Chairman,
Halloran Associates, Florida, USA

"With the looming climate crisis and rapid loss of nature, the production and consumption of goods must adopt principles of sustainability and circularity intending to achieve a net zero, nature-positive and pollution-free world. To make sound policy and investment decisions on technology solutions in this pursuit, it is vital to have practical decision-making tools that can enable smart choices. More specifically, understanding the comprehensive economic implications of the available and emerging solutions is vital to ensure that positive and negative externalities are factored in while investing in these solutions. Life Cycle Cost Analysis is a useful decision tool in this context and I am pleased that Nirjhar's book explores the application of this tool in great depth yet in an approach that can be understood easily by learners, practitioners, and decision-makers. He illustrates the Life Cycle Cost Analysis methodologies meticulously.

"For learners, the book allows understanding the concepts of Life Cycle Cost Analysis. At the same time, it can trigger practitioners and decision-makers to review and reinvent the concepts of Life Cycle Cost Analysis and its methodologies. Simplistic innovative mathematical steps and newer concepts of calculating Present Value will be catalytic in this context. The methodologies explained in the book are universal. It is incredible to know that some companies have already integrated some of these methodologies into their Life Cycle Cost Analysis model. It shows the novelty and agility of the methodologies illustrated by Nirjhar to influence real-time applications. Being a professional in the climate and sustainability space myself, I am glad that his book on Life Cycle Cost Analysis has a strong focus on sustainability solutions with specific examples of clean technology solutions demonstrated in the book. After his book on Digital Transformation: A Strategic Structure for Implementation, this book is another grand effort by him to contribute to sustainable development."

Aloke Barnwal, Lead- Sustainable Cities; Senior Climate Change Specialist- Adaptation (LDCF, SCCF), USA

"Nirjhar Chakravorti's book offers a unique exploration of business economics with untapped potential. Nirjhar delves into the world of economic institutions involved in production and sales, operating within a dynamic socio-economic environment.

"The sustainability of a business relies on the ability to earn profits by meeting customer needs. To achieve this, businesses must enhance efficiency, adapt to changing market conditions, improve customer experiences, and add value to their lives. Profit, in this context, refers to the surplus of revenue from the sale of products and services over the total costs incurred during a specific period. Managing costs effectively requires the application of engineering economics principles to estimate, analyze, and control costs throughout the lifespan of a product or project. These principles and techniques are relevant to both product development and project execution. In addition to this, the buying and selling process plays a vital role in any business. Traditionally, buyers, in majority, consider the purchase price when assessing alternatives. However, in recent decades, there has been an increased awareness of recurring costs incurred by an asset over its lifespan. This combination of purchase cost and recurring costs, referred to as life cycle cost or total cost of ownership, has garnered attention within businesses.

"Recurring costs have long-term implications, especially in the face of fluctuating energy sources and imbalances between skilled labour and technology, which impact operational costs. In this evolving landscape, Life Cycle Cost Analysis serves as a decision-making tool that helps synchronize divisions by focusing on facts, money, and time.

"As a result, Nirjhar Chakravorti's book on Life Cycle Cost Analysis is timely and offers valuable insights for professionals and academics alike. His straightforward methodologies, illustrated through various case studies, provide a useful framework for making critical business decisions."

Dr. Ani Oganesyan, Associate Professor at Peoples' Friendship University of Russia (RUDN University), Russia

"LCCA is an economic tool which sums up the total cost of ownership. In a sustainable business environment, Life Cycle Cost Analysis is becoming an important tool. By using LCCA, various aspects of a business can be evaluated, including decisions on taking up new projects. For project management, LCCA is still in the nascent stage and yet to be explored to its fullest capacity. Nirjhar Chakravorti has unveiled the areas where LCCA can be effectively used as part of Project Management. It is fascinating that the book explained how LCCA can be applied as complementary or supplementary to traditional financial analysis as part of project decision making. Also, various other aspects such as make-or-buy decision or project delay analysis using LCCA are also narrated in the book, which provides a new dimension to project management. The unique part of the book is the simple methodology used for LCCA, which can be adopted as a universal framework."

Tassos Tsochataridis, MSc, PMP, Project Management Professional, Civil Engineer, Greece

"This book by Nirjhar Chakravorti is an indispensable guide for anyone involved in project management, regional development, or sustainability efforts. As a project manager in regional development in Austria, I have seen firsthand the transformative power of Life Cycle Cost Analysis (LCCA) in shaping sustainable and economically sound decisions. Nirjhar

Chakravorti's book offers a profound understanding of LCCA, making it a must-read for those eager to secure a brighter future for our planet and our economies.

"In today's world, where sustainability is at the forefront of our collective consciousness, LCCA is a critical tool in the arsenal of decision-makers. This book introduces readers to the concept of LCCA and provides a comprehensive methodology that can be applied across diverse applications. Chakravorti's straightforward and accessible approach ensures that both professionals and researchers can grasp the complexities of life cycle costing without unnecessary jargon or complexity.

"One of the key takeaways from this book is the realization that the cost of an asset doesn't stop at its initial acquisition and installation. The cumulative operating costs, environmental considerations, and even the cost of disposal are integral parts of the equation. LCCA takes these factors into account, providing a holistic view of the economic implications of any decision. What sets this book apart is its recognition of the growing importance of environmental costs, such as carbon emissions and health impacts. Nirjhar Chakravorti's expertise shines through in every chapter, and his ability to demystify complex economic concepts is commendable. He also introduces a unique methodology for considering the impact of inflation over time, adding a valuable dimension to the LCCA process."

Alexandra C. M. Katzian, Project Manager at LEADER Region Südliches Waldviertel – Nibelungengau, Austria

Life Cycle Cost Analysis

Life Cycle Costing (LCC) is the process of economic analysis to assess the total cost of ownership of an asset, including its cost of procurement, installation, operation, maintenance, conversion, and decommissioning.

The economic approach to assess the total cost of owning an asset or facility is known as Life Cycle Cost Analysis (LCCA). LCCA is a key economic tool for business decision-making in terms of various functional requirements, such as sustainability, asset management, supply chain management, and project management.

Every organization is a combination of various interrelated functions or departments. Every function has its own set of objectives and targets. Even though all functions try to achieve overall organizational objectives, in reality, they work to protect their functional interests as well. In many cases, it becomes detrimental to the health of the organization. This conflicting behavior increases when decisions are made on subjective considerations. When a company's strategy works on an objective platform, chances of conflict are reduced. LCCA can be used as a management decision tool for synchronizing functional conflicts by focusing on facts, money, and time.

Life Cycle Cost Analysis: An Economic Model for Sustainable Tomorrow explains a simple, innovative model to carry out LCCA, along with a unique methodology to determine how the value of money changes over a period of time.

Life Cycle Cost Analysis

An Economic Model for Sustainable Tomorrow

Nirjhar Chakravorti

Routledge
Taylor & Francis Group

A PRODUCTIVITY PRESS BOOK

First published 2024
by Routledge
605 Third Avenue, New York, NY 10158

and by Routledge
4 Park Square, Milton Park, Abingdon, Oxon, OX14 4RN

Routledge is an imprint of the Taylor & Francis Group, an informa business

© 2024 Nirjhar Chakravorti

ISBN: 978-1-032-61167-9 (hbk)
ISBN: 978-1-032-61166-2 (pbk)
ISBN: 978-1-003-46233-0 (ebk)

DOI: 10.4324/9781003462330

Typeset in Minion
by Deanta Global Publishing Services, Chennai, India

Contents

Acknowledgements

I am immensely grateful to Dr. David G. Halloran, Chairman and Founder of Icon Associates, Chicago, Illinois, USA for his continuous support and encouragement.

I would like to express my thankfulness to Sanya Mathura (Author and Managing Director, Strategic Reliability Solutions Ltd, Trinidad & Tobago), Arianna Amati (Senior Project Manager from Italy), Ritu Kesarwani (Consultant and Educator for Circular Economy & LCA, USA), and Tassos Tsochataridis (Project Manager, Greece) for their valuable input. I must mention the extensive support received from Marcel Smit (LCCA Expert and Senior Research Scientist at TNO, Netherlands). Also, I would like to express my gratitude to Dr. Ani Oganesyan (Associate Professor at the Peoples' Friendship University of Russia) and Alexandra Katzian (Project Manager at LEADER Region Südliches Waldviertel – Nibelungengau, Austria) for their support.

I am sincerely thankful to Dr. Amaresh Dalal (Professor, IIT Guwahati, India), Dr. Amitava Ray (Principal, Jalpaiguri Government Engineering College, India), and Dr. Apurba Shee (Associate Professor of Applied Economics, Natural Resources Institute, University of Greenwich, UK) for their encouragement.

I would like to express my immense gratitude to all the members of the Jalpaiguri Government Engineering College Alumni Association, JGEC Campus, Jalpaiguri, India for their support in implementing various concepts that helped me in writing the book.

I would like to express my sincere gratitude to my organization, Tata Consulting Engineers Ltd (TCE), for providing an environment of innovation. I would like to provide special thanks to my colleagues at TCE, Sushil Rawat (Associate Vice President) and Sankar Lal Bandyopadhyay (Consultant), for their continuous support. I would like to thanks to Biswajit Bhattacharya (Associate Vice President) and Kaustav Das (General Manager) for their encouragement. Also, I must mention the names of Dr. Rajashekhar R Malur (Senior Vice President) and Shantanu Shantaram Apte (Vice President) for their inspiration.

I would like to provide special thanks to my friends and colleagues Dr. Debdeep Sikdar, Pralay Chand Ghosh, Aloke Barnwal, Rajib Bhattacharya, Ramu Chalumuri, Saran Khan, Subir Ghosh, Bidyut Jyoti Chatterjee, Amy Bruton Bailey, and George Bailey for their support.

I would like to express my gratitude to my wife Shipra, my daughters Samriddhi and Souriti, and all the family members for their support and encouragement.

I would like to remember my parents, the late Manabendra Nath Chakrabarty and the late Maya Chakrabarty, for their immense contributions to nurturing my thought process driven by innovation and out-of-the-box thinking that aided me in conceptualizing the principles crucial to my book.

Author's Biography

Nirjhar Chakravorti was born and raised in the small historical town of Murshidabad in eastern India, in an ambience influenced by communism. During his graduation in Mechanical Engineering from Jalpaiguri Government Engineering College at the foothills of the Himalayas, he was exposed to organizational strategy and an open market economy inspired by innovation and holistic growth. He was fascinated by the correlation between economic principles and engineering applications. In his professional career, he has always focused on applying economic principles in the analysis of engineering decisions to ensure business sustainability. He was first exposed to the concept of Life Cycle Cost Analysis at an early stage of his professional career when he was part of a Total Productive Maintenance (TPM) team. He developed an innovative model for Life Cycle Cost Analysis and evaluation of the present value of money. Since then, the model has been used in various applications. The beauty of the model is the simplicity that makes it appealing to business leaders, as well as working-level professionals, even without an extensive knowledge of economics.

Nirjhar Chakravorti is a strategic thinker. He is the author of the highly acclaimed book *Digital Transformation: A Strategic Structure for Implementation*, published by Taylor & Francis. Nirjhar is a leader who is focused on the implementation of sustainability strategies. He has extensively used the Life Cycle Cost Analysis concept as a sustainability tool for various applications across industries.

Introduction

For years, we have focused on two main drivers while making procurement decisions for any tangible or intangible asset. The first is the design of the asset in terms of functional requirements, aesthetics, and comfort of use. The second factor is the cost of acquisition and installation, and the realization of the asset. A third factor that has recently begun to gain greater awareness is the operating cost of the asset in use. The operating cost includes operations, maintenance, repair, and replacement costs. It has been observed that in most cases, the cumulative operating cost is significantly high over a period of time compared to the initial procurement and installation cost. In addition, users are concerned with the cost of disposal and the residual value of a property at the end of its use. The sum of the initial and operating costs of an asset, including all other associated costs throughout its useful life, is known as Life Cycle Cost. It can also be termed as Total Cost of Ownership.

Life Cycle Cost Analysis (LCCA) is an economic approach used to assess the total cost of owning an asset or facility. The LCCA concept has grown in popularity as awareness of the cost of ownership increases. With the growing awareness of environmental costs, including carbon and health costs, the importance of LCCA is increasing dramatically.

This book illustrates the concept and methodology of the LCCA. The methodology described in this book is a simple arithmetic model which can be used by all for any application. Also, this book explains a unique methodology to demonstrate how the value of money changes over a period of time when inflation plays a major role. This book provides working knowledge to all professionals and researchers on how to analyze life cycle costs and prepare the LCCA report. This book explains why LCCA is a key economic tool for business decision-making in terms of sustainability, asset management, supply chain management, and project management.

DOI: 10.4324/9781003462330-1

Initial acquisition and installation costs are said to be the tip of the iceberg for the entire Life Cycle Cost of an asset. To make the right decision to acquire an asset, a thorough analysis must be done to assess the life cycle cost of owning the asset. It is time to understand the Life-Cycle Costing process and implement it in a simplistic and logical manner so that all stakeholders are on the same page.

1

Overview

A business is an economic institution related to the production and sales of goods and services that operates in a dynamic socio-economic environment. The sustainability of a business depends on earning profit by satisfying customer's needs. The business needs to enhance efficiency, transform products, and change ways of working with changing market scenarios, enhance customer's experience, and add value to customer's life to ensure profit. Profit is the excess of total revenue received from the sale of products and services over the total cost of all inputs used during a specific period of time (Figure 1.1).

In financial terms, revenue depends on the selling price of products or services or projects.

In short, revenue is the multiplication of the unit selling price and number of items sold. The selling price is mostly market determined which depends on the dynamics of supply and demand. As businesses do not have much control over the selling price in a competitive market, the focus is on cost. The less the cost, the more the profit. This is the simple mantra for profit maximization. That is the reason managing cost is of utmost importance to the business.

To successfully manage costs, it is necessary to apply engineering economics principles for cost estimation, analysis, and control throughout the product or project lifespan. This approach helps an organization to manage costs for its products, services, or projects. Cost engineering principles and techniques are applicable to both product development and project execution.

For both product and project, the major components of cost engineering are as follows:

DOI: 10.4324/9781003462330-2

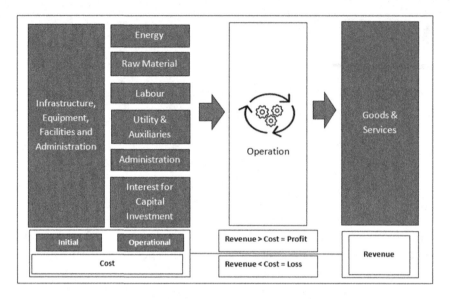

FIGURE 1.1
Business cost model

- Cost estimation and analysis to review profitability at different phases of product development or project execution, based on design maturity.
- Budgeting at the final stage of the design prior to execution.
- Cost control during execution.
- An economic evaluation of project execution or product development, during implementation and afterwards.

WHAT IS THE DIFFERENCE BETWEEN A PRODUCT AND A PROJECT?

A project is a one-of-a-kind, temporary endeavour with a start and end that consists of a series of actions intended to accomplish a certain goal, generally the development of a good or service. A project is not a usual operation of any business.

A product, on the other hand, is a good, service, system, platform, or application that is created, usually for sale, to suit the demands of customers and businesses. A project can be taken up to build a product.

Cost estimation is primarily referred to as the estimation of initial cost or capital expenditure (CAPEX). However, in addition to initial cost, people are becoming interested in knowing the operational cost during the useful life cycle of the asset or product or service as well. That is why calculating operational cost or OPEX is becoming an important aspect of cost engineering. In addition to that one more aspect that is becoming significant is to understand the total cost incurred by the asset or product or service throughout its life cycle which is popularly known as Life Cycle Cost. This concept of Life Cycle Cost helps in evaluating multiple options and selecting the most optimized option. Also, by using this concept, the payback period can be evaluated for the selected option. This is a critical part of engineering economics.

ENGINEERING ECONOMICS

Engineering economics is a branch of economics that deals with the application of economic concepts to the study of engineering decisions. It applies microeconomic theories in a simplified manner with the help of mathematical and statistical tools.

Time value of money is one of the important factors for engineering economics whereas demand/supply, price determination, and competition are considered to be fixed inputs from other sources. Engineering economics offers various advantages as it allows industry professionals to make strategic decisions for their companies. While financial skills are key to the company's operations, the engineering economy provides a decision-making framework. Engineering economics is the study of the economic merits of proposed technical solutions. It helps to establish the long-term viability of a decision by evaluating a cost-benefit analysis.

Cost engineering is part of engineering economics. Cost engineering is concerned with project cost management, which includes tasks such as estimating, cost control, cost forecasting, risk analysis, and so on.

2

Purpose of Life Cycle Cost Analysis

Life Cycle Cost Analysis (LCCA) is the process of economic analysis to evaluate the entire cost of possession of an entity, including its cost of installation, operation, maintenance, replacement, and decommissioning. LCCA is an economic tool that combines both engineering art and science to make logical business decisions. The entity can be a product, system, facility, or project.

LCCA provides important inputs in the decision-making for the design, development, and use of an entity. This is more widely used for the selection of a process, system, or product when various alternatives are available. LCCA can be used by either suppliers or by end users, based on their requirements. By using LCCA, end users can evaluate and compare alternative products, systems, facilities, or projects. Also, with the help of LCCA, end users can assess the economic viability of a decision. On the other hand, by using Life Cycle Cost, suppliers can optimize their design by evaluating alternatives and by performing trade-off studies. LCCA also helps suppliers to evaluate various operating and maintenance cost strategies.

The Life Cycle Cost of an entity can be analyzed for the following purposes:

Study of alternatives (relative analysis)
Planning and budgeting of an investment (absolute analysis)

While absolute analysis looks at an entity's inherent cost without comparing it to others, relative analysis is based on the costs of similar entities.

DOI: 10.4324/9781003462330-3

WHY LCCA IS USED?

Different departments in a company typically have competing interests which are conflicting many times. A typical conflict between the objectives of different functions within a company is as follows:

Project Engineering wants to minimize investment costs,
Production Engineering wants to maximize operation hours,
Maintenance Engineering wants to minimize repair hours,
Reliability Engineering wants to nullify failures,
Accounting wants to maximize the project's net present value,
Shareholders want to increase stockholder wealth.

LCCA can be used as a management decision tool for synchronizing divisional conflicts by focusing on the following factors:

- Facts
- Money
- Time.

LCCA is used for different applications depending on the requirement. Nowadays, almost all types of organizations are using LCCA as part of the business decision-making process. LCCA provides an opportunity to validate decisions from an economic point of view. With the growing focus on sustainability, the importance of LCCA is increasing as well, because it helps to monetize the environmentally detrimental effects for using it as part of evaluation.

LCC has been extensively followed as a formal and applied discipline in the United States since the 1960s. The US Department of Defence encouraged the development and use of LCC to improve the cost-effectiveness of competitive awards.

The use of LCC has extended beyond defence systems to other areas of public sector, industrial and consumer products. The scope of LCC has expanded in tandem with this trend in different areas, such as construction materials, machine tools, and automobile parts.

For the purpose of increasing their capital productivity, all sectors of our economy are becoming more cost-conscious. In the past, it has tended to be true to make the traditional claim that procurement costs and physical performance metrics are what ultimately determine procurement decisions. Life Cycle Costs are gaining importance across all sectors, according to current trends. More than ever before, the government, business, service, and consumer sectors are using LCC ideas. In recent times, life cycle pricing has gained popularity, particularly in the context of sustainable construction. In industrial applications, there is a push to include the concept of LCCA. National governments and certification bodies across the globe are emphasizing the use of LCCA. Many organizations are focusing on embedding LCCA in the strategic decision-making process. For example, the Water and Sanitation Programme (WSP) management has included LCCA in strategic decision-making. WSP is managed by the World Bank, which collaborated with governments, funders, academics, civil society, and the business sector to ensure that poor people have inexpensive, safe, and long-term access to water and sanitation services. WSP worked in a number of African, East Asian, Latin American and Caribbean, and South Asian nations. The WSP has implemented LCCA on a large scale.

3
Life Cycle Cost Analysis Methodology

For an asset, there are two major cost elements:

a) Initial Cost (IC), i.e., CAPEX
b) Operation and Maintenance Cost (OC), i.e., OPEX

The cost elements need to be identified and further divided based on the purpose and scope of the Life Cycle Cost Analysis (LCCA) study. The major components of cost elements are provided in Table 3.1.

During the decision-making process for acquiring an asset, various alternatives are explored. As part of the LCCA, these cost elements for all the options are calculated for the intended life span and further analyzed.

STEPS FOR LCCA

The steps for the computation of LCCA are as follows (refer to Figure 3.1):

- Determination of the life cycle
- Valuation of each cost element
- Calculation of the present value of each element
- Calculation of LCCA
- Analysis of the results

TABLE 3.1

Major Cost Elements for an Asset

Elements of Initial Cost (CAPEX)	Elements of Operation and Maintenance Cost (OPEX)
• Design and development cost • Investment on asset, or cost of equipment and land acquisition (if applicable) • Installation cost or erection and commission cost • Indirect cost such as temporary facilities.	• Labour cost • Energy cost • Spare and maintenance costs • Raw material cost.

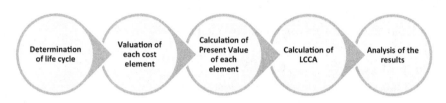

FIGURE 3.1
Steps for computation of LCCA

Step 1: Determine the Life Cycle Time Frame

In LCCA, life cycle means the life of a particular asset that is in operation. It refers to the time between the two selected dates over which the cost analysis will be carried out. This time frame may or may not represent the time between cradle to grave. Cradle to grave refers to the period between raw material acquisition to build an asset to the final disposal of the asset. Rather this time frame can be decided based on specific performance requirements under which the assessment needs to be carried out. The supplier of any asset provides the life cycle depending on design calculation and experience. Based on the supplier's data, the end user decides the Life Cycle, i.e., how long the customer wants to use the asset. Planning, acquisition, usage, maintenance, and disposal are the five major stages of an asset's life cycle. The usage and maintenance stages will consume the majority of the asset's lifetime. While calculating the life cycle period, the end user considers the effect of the maintenance facility, technological obsolescence, and economic uncertainty factor, as well. After that, the end user decides the cycle time of the asset and subsequently period for each element of LCCA. For example, say, a company decides that the total life cycle of the product will be ten years from the fund allocation, among which the first year will be the initial cost zone and the remaining nine years will be under the operation and maintenance cost zone.

The Life of an asset is not similar to the conventional concept of the Product Life Cycle. The conventional concept of the Product Life Cycle implies the period based on the demand for the product in the market, starting from the launch of the product up to the time when the company withdraw the product from the market. The conventional Product Life Cycle is purely a marketing concept, whereas cycle time in LCCA is the life of a particular asset in operation.

Step 2: Valuation of Cost Elements

Estimation of the monetary value for each cost element is one of the most important steps of LCCA. The initial cost is normally a single-time expenditure for any asset which is known as CAPEX. Operation and Maintenance costs are incurred regularly throughout the asset life cycle which is commonly referred to as OPEX. Operation and Maintenance Cost elements are calculated on an annual basis. The Operation and Maintenance Cost elements are future costs which shall be incurred every year.

EXAMPLE OF MAJOR COST ELEMENTS

Initial Cost:

Examples of some of the typical initial costs are design and development costs, land and office space acquisition costs, equipment costs, erection and commissioning costs, etc.

Design and Development Cost:

The cost of design and development mostly depends on the effort put into it. The design and development cost includes the direct cost of designing the asset and the other peripheral engineering cost such as consultant engagement from concept to commissioning.

Land and Office Space Acquisition Costs:

If the purchase of land or office is involved, then land or office space acquisition cost needs to be considered as the initial cost.

Equipment Cost:

Equipment costs include the cost of material, manufacturing/fabrication, transportation, etc. for a product. This cost component includes labour costs involved in the manufacturing of the product. Also, in case the asset is a bought-out item, then the engineering cost of the asset can also be part of the equipment costs.

Erection and Commissioning Cost:

Erection expenses are the costs associated with the product's installation. It is a capital expenditure which includes labour costs associated with erection. If the installation of the product needs dismantling of any existing facilities, the same also needs to be considered under Initial Cost. All other installation-related costs such as scaffolding, crane, tools and tackles, special dresses for installation, associated travel cost, etc. as applicable come under erection cost.

Commissioning cost is the cost of authorizing a facility to operate. These include fuel or raw material costs, team costs, review costs, labour costs involved in commissioning activities, and so on.

OPERATION AND MAINTENANCE COST

Operation and Maintenance Costs vary from time to time. So, they are more of an estimate. These estimates, however, provide useful information about long-term costs associated with an asset, equipment, or system.

Examples of some of the typical Operation and Maintenance Costs are labour costs, energy costs, spare and maintenance costs, material costs, etc. which are related to operation and maintenance.

After a certain time, specific portions of an asset may need to be replaced. Assumption and estimation of the component replacement cost is an important aspect of LCCA.

The disposal cost of assets after the end of life or utilization needs to be considered as part of Life Cycle Cost estimation.

Replacement and disposal costs, as applicable, are not recurring costs. They can be considered as separate cost entities in addition to Operation and Maintenance Costs.

In recent times, annual carbon cost has been also considered to capture the effect of pollution and greenhouse gas generation by any product or process or system. The cost of generating carbon footprint, if applicable, comes under OPEX category which has an immense sustainability impact.

Step 3: Calculation of Present Value (PV) of Each Cost Element

The money available today is worth more than that in the future. Today's 100 dollars is worth more than the 100 dollars after five years. The primary reason behind this concept is the "earning capacity" of money. So, after five years if someone earns 100 USD then what shall be the present value of that 100 USD? Few methods are already available for the economic and financial evaluation of present value for any future value or future cost.

The present value of future income or future cost can be calculated by using a discounting factor. The discount rate is an interest rate a central bank charges depository institutions that borrow reserves from it. For example, let's say Mr Ram expects 1000 USD in one year's time. To determine the present value of this 1000 USD, Ram would need to discount it by a particular rate of interest (often the risk-free rate but not always). Assuming a discount rate of 10%, the 1000 USD in a year's time would be equivalent to 909.09 USD to Ram today (i.e., 1000/[1+0.10]). The discount rate is referred to as the real discount rate when the present value (PV) is determined simply by taking the effect of the discount rate into account (refer to Equation 3.1).

$$PV = \frac{C}{\left(1 + \dfrac{d}{100}\right)^n} \qquad (3.1)$$

Where,

  C = any cost element at the nth year.
  d = discount rate.

The discount rate is not the sole element influencing the present value of any future costs in the real-world market environment. Another significant factor that influences present value is inflation. The modified discount rate becomes the nominal discount rate when the discount rate is changed in relation to the inflation rate. The inflation rate is the percentage by which prices of goods and services rise beyond their average levels. It is the rate by which the purchasing power of the people in a particular geography declines in a specified period.

The present value of future income or cost can be calculated using the formula provided in Equation 3.2.

$$PV = \frac{C\left(1+\dfrac{i}{100}\right)^{n-1}}{\left(1+\dfrac{d}{100}\right)^{n}} \qquad (3.2)$$

Where,

  C = any cost element at the nth year.
  d = discount rate.
  i = inflation rate.

The use of the inflation rate as indicated in Equation 3.2 is a more logical approach for calculating present value, as inflation significantly influences monetary value.

The present value of each cost element needs to be calculated by using Equation 3.2.

Note: There are other established formulas as well for calculating present value by using the inflation rate. However, in this book, Equation 3.2 is used for calculating the present value.

DISCOUNT RATE

The discount rate is equivalent to an interest rate, which is used in calculating the present value of future cash flows. The discount rate is used to determine the value of certain future cash flows today.

Therefore, from an investor's point of view, the discount rate is an important parameter for comparing the value of cash flows.

DIFFERENCE BETWEEN INTEREST RATE AND DISCOUNT RATE

The interest rate is the amount charged by a bank or financial institute (lender) to an individual (borrower) for the use of assets. On the other hand, the discount rate is the interest rate that the Federal Reserve Bank charges to the financial institutions and banks on its overnight loans.

Interest rates depend on various factors such as the risk associated with lending, the borrower's creditworthiness, etc. On the contrary, the discount rate can be considered as the average rate that the Federal Reserve Banks would charge to other banks and financial institutions.

The discount rate is steadier in consideration as it is not governed by demand and supply in the economy, whereas interest rates are affected by demand and supply in the economy.

INFLATION RATE

One of the most widely used terms in economics is inflation. It measures the rate of increase in the price of a group of products and services over a predetermined time frame, usually a year. The consumer price index (CPI) is a tool for measuring inflation. CPI keeps the economy healthy at low rates. Yet, when the rate of inflation rises quickly, it can have a negative impact on the economy through lowering buying power, increasing interest rates, slowing economic development, and other factors.

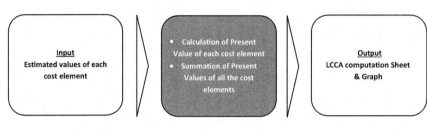

FIGURE 3.2
LCCA calculation method

Step 4: Calculation of Life Cycle Cost

After the calculation of PVs of all the cost elements for each year over the life cycle of the entity, the PVs of each year are added to calculate the yearly values of Life Cycle Cost (refer to Figure 3.2).

After calculating the Life Cycle Cost of the second year, the same is added to the first year's Life Cycle Cost to arrive at cumulative Life Cycle Cost after the second year. Similarly, the third year's Life Cycle Cost is added to the cumulative Life Cycle Cost of the second year. Likewise, every year's Life Cycle Cost is added to the cumulative Life Cycle Cost of the previous years so that the total Life Cycle Cost of any entity is derived from its life cycle period. Each year's cumulative Life Cycle Cost values are plotted in a graph.

Step 5: Analysis of the Results

If one entity needs to be selected among multiple options, then Life Cycle Cost is calculated for every entity. Data for every entity are analyzed, and the entity having the lowest Life Cycle Cost becomes one of the preferred options. However, the lowest Life Cycle Cost option may not necessarily be accepted always as other considerations such as risks, available budgets, and political and environmental concerns are other major factors for making the right decision.

There are various methodologies of LCCA which are in use to predict the Life Cycle Cost. Many of the LCCA methodologies involve knowledge of advanced mathematics as well. However, one thing is very clear: the market economy is dynamic. Nobody can predict when a war can change market conditions or when a pandemic can suddenly stall the global economy. In view of the same, simpler economic tools can be effective to provide a reasonable insight into a business decision, instead of investing an enormous amount of time and effort in calculating an economic output. This is more applicable when options are compared with the same economic assumptions.

In today's business scenario, there is a need for quick decision-making to leverage the opportunities embraced by innovation and disruptions. In this aspect, design thinking is one of the major drivers for business decision-making. For quantitative decision-making, businesses started implementing modern tools like machine learning. Other qualitative tools such as Strength, Weakness, Opportunity and Threat (SWOT) analysis, fishbone diagram, etc. are in use for decision-making as well. For financial decision-making, CAPEX estimation and financial analysis are conventional tools along with the calculation of economic ratios. In this context, a simpler LCCA methodology can be an effective tool which provides a holistic economic overview for business decision-making.

Also, sensitivity analysis can be done as part of risk management to predict Life Cycle Costs in changing variable scenarios. During sensitivity analysis, different sets of calculations are done by altering major variables such as discount rate, inflation rate, energy cost, etc.

4

Case Study for Life Cycle Cost Analysis

A steel fabrication shop has one sophisticated computer numerical control (CNC)-operated sheet metal cutting machine. Due to increasing demand, the owner decided to expand the business by installing three more sheet metal cutting machines.

For new machines, there are two options:

Option 1: Sophisticated CNC machines, or

Option 2: Semi-automated machines.

OPTION 1

Initial Cost

Depending upon the stage of the project, Initial Cost (IC) or Capital Expenditure (CAPEX) needs to be estimated for procuring three new Sophisticated CNC machines.

For the Case Study, the summary of the Initial Cost estimate for option 1 is as per Table 4.1.

Computation of Present Value for IC

The total IC of 52.90 million USD will be invested in the first 12 months. Present value (PV) of the Total Initial Cost shall be calculated by using Equation 3.2 as follows:

DOI: 10.4324/9781003462330-5

$$PV = \frac{IC\left(1+\dfrac{i}{100}\right)^{n-1}}{\left(1+\dfrac{d}{100}\right)^{n}}$$

n is the year on which PV will be calculated. For this purpose, $n = 1$ year, and the estimated discount rate (d) and inflation rate (i) are 8% and 5%, respectively. Considering the same, PV for the Initial Cost of option 1 can be calculated as follows:

$$PV = \frac{52.90\left(1+\dfrac{5}{100}\right)^{0}}{\left(1+\dfrac{8}{100}\right)^{1}}$$

$$= 48.98 \text{ million USD}$$

Operation and Maintenance Cost

For the Case Study, the summary of Operation and Maintenance Cost (OC) or Operational Expenditure (OPEX) sheet for option 1 is as per Table 4.2.

TABLE 4.1

Initial Cost Estimate for Option 1

	Initial Cost		
Cost Element	**Value (in Million USD)**	**Time Phase**	**Remarks**
Design and development (D)	0.00	–	Included in Manufacturing and Supply Cost as it is bought out item
Investment in asset (Manufacturing and Supply) (A)	46.40	0–1 year	From project initiation point, the equipment will be installed within 1 year time, so the time span for IC is kept between 0 and 1 year
Installation and Project Management (I)	6.50	0–1 year	
Total Initial Cost (IC)	52.90	0–1 year	

TABLE 4.2

Operation and Maintenance Cost Estimate for Option 1

	Operation and Maintenance Cost		
Cost Element	Value (in Million USD)/Year	Time Phase	Remarks
Labour (L)	0.20	2–10 years	No labour
Energy (E)	5.00	2–10 years	Management Information
Spare and maintenance (S)	3.20	2–10 years	System (MIS) report of
Raw material (M)	30.20		existing equipment, as new proposed equipment will be identical
Total Operation and Maintenance Cost (OC)	38.60	2–10 years	

Computation of Present Value for OC

As per the project plan, the machines are going to be installed within a year from the project initiation. Hence, the Operation and Maintenance Cost (OC) is going to be incurred from the second year till the end of the estimated life cycle of the machine, i.e., 10 years. For calculation purposes, it is assumed that the OC of 38.60 million USD as per today's value shall be incurred every year. PV of 38.60 million USD is to be calculated every year using Equation 3.2.

PV of OC at nth year shall be as follows:

$$PV = \frac{OC\left(1 + \dfrac{i}{100}\right)^{n-1}}{\left(1 + \dfrac{d}{100}\right)^{n}}$$

Considering estimated discount rate (d) and inflation rate (i) of 8% and 5%, respectively, PV in the nth year is as follows:

$$PV = \frac{38.60\left(1 + \dfrac{5}{100}\right)^{n-1}}{\left(1 + \dfrac{8}{100}\right)^{n}}$$

TABLE 4.3

LCC Calculation for Option 1

	Factors		Operation and Maintenance Cost (OC)				
Time Period	Dis- counting Factor	Inflation Factor	Future OC at nth Year	PV of Any Year	Total PV Incurred	PV of Initial Cost (IC)	Total LCC
nth Year	$1/(1+8/100)^n$	$(1+5/100)^{(n-1)}$	USD	USD	USD	USD	USD
A	B	C	D	E = D × B × C	F=E + Last Year's F	G	H = G + F
1	0.93	1	0	0	0	48.98	48.98
2	0.86	1.05	38.60	34.75	34.75	48.98	83.73
3	0.79	1.10	38.60	33.78	68.53	48.98	117.51
4	0.74	1.16	38.60	32.84	101.37	48.98	150.36
5	0.68	1.22	38.60	31.93	133.31	48.98	182.29
6	0.63	1.28	38.60	31.04	164.35	48.98	213.33
7	0.58	1.34	38.60	30.18	194.53	48.98	243.52
8	0.54	1.41	38.60	29.34	223.88	48.98	272.86
9	0.50	1.48	38.60	28.53	252.41	48.98	301.39
10	0.46	1.55	38.60	27.74	280.14	48.98	329.13

All costs are in million USD

For example, PV in second year will be 34.75 million USD, by using $n = 2$. Likewise, the PV of OC needs to be calculated every year.

Computation of Life Cycle Cost

The Life Cycle Cost sheet is prepared as per Table 4.3, by calculating the yearly PV of IC and OC. The formulas for the calculation are also provided in the table.

OPTION 2

Initial Cost (IC)

Depending upon the stage of the project, Initial Cost or CAPEX needs to be calculated for option 2.

For the Case Study, the summary of the Initial Cost estimate for option 2 is provided in Table 4.4.

TABLE 4.4

Initial Cost Estimate for Option 2

	Initial Cost		
Cost Element	**Value (in Million USD)**	**Time Phase**	**Remarks**
Design and development (D)	0.00	–	Included in Manufacturing and Supply Cost as it is bought out item
Investment in asset (Manufacturing and Supply) (A)	23.40	0–1 year	From project initiation point, the equipment will be installed within 1 year time, so time span
Installation and Project Management (I)	4.50	0–1 year	for IC is kept between 0 and 1 year time
Total Initial Cost (IC)	27.90	0–1 year	

Computation of Present Value for IC

The total IC of 27.90 million USD will be invested in the 12th month from project initiation. PV of the Total Initial Cost shall be calculated using the following concept:

$$PV = \frac{IC\left(1+\dfrac{i}{100}\right)^{n-1}}{\left(1+\dfrac{d}{100}\right)^{n}}$$

n is the year on which PV will be calculated. For this purpose, $n = 1$ year, and the estimated discount rate (d) and inflation rate (i) are 8% and 5%, respectively. Considering the same, PV for the Initial Cost of option 2 can be calculated as follows:

$$PV = \frac{27.90\left(1+\dfrac{5}{100}\right)^{0}}{\left(1+\dfrac{8}{100}\right)^{1}}$$

$$= 25.83 \text{ million USD}$$

TABLE 4.5

Operation and Maintenance Cost Estimate for Option 2

	Operation and Maintenance Cost		
Cost Element	Value (in Million USD)/ Year	Time Phase	Remarks
Labour (L)	1.50	2–10 years	Data collected from
Energy (E)	8.00	2–10 years	equipment supplier's
Spare and maintenance (S)	6.00	2–10 years	catalogue, offer, and
Raw material (M)	37.75	2–10 years	market survey
Total Operation and Maintenance Cost (OC)	53.25	2–10 years	

Operation and Maintenance Cost (OC)

For Case Study 1, the summary of Operation and Maintenance Cost or OPEX sheet for option 2 is as per Table 4.5.

Computation of Present Value for OC

The estimated yearly Operation and Maintenance Cost (OC) for option 2 as per today's market condition is calculated as 53.25 million USD. PV of OC needs to be calculated for every year.

PV of OC at nth year shall be as follows:

$$PV = \frac{53.25\left(1+\dfrac{i}{100}\right)^{n-1}}{\left(1+\dfrac{d}{100}\right)^{n}}$$

Considering estimated discount rate (d) and inflation rate (i) of 8% and 5%, respectively, PV in the nth year is as follows:

$$PV = \frac{53.25\left(1+\dfrac{5}{100}\right)^{n-1}}{\left(1+\dfrac{8}{100}\right)^{n}}$$

TABLE 4.6

LCC Calculation for Option 2

	Factors		Operation and Maintenance Cost (OC)				
Time Period	Dis-Counting Factor	Inflation Factor	Future OC in nth Year	PV of Any Year	Total PV Incurred	PV of Initial Cost (IC)	Total LCC
nth Year	$1/(1+8/100)^n$	$(1+5/100)^{(n-1)}$	USD	USD	USD	USD	USD
A	B	C	D	$E = D \times B \times C$	$F = E + $ Last Year's F	G	$H = G + F$
1	0.93	1	0	0	0	25.83	25.83
2	0.86	1.05	53.25	47.94	47.94	25.83	73.77
3	0.79	1.10	53.25	46.60	94.54	25.83	120.37
4	0.74	1.16	53.25	45.31	139.85	25.83	165.68
5	0.68	1.22	53.25	44.05	183.90	25.83	209.73
6	0.63	1.28	53.25	42.83	226.73	25.83	252.56
7	0.58	1.34	53.25	41.64	268.37	25.83	294.20
8	0.54	1.41	53.25	40.48	308.85	25.83	334.68
9	0.50	1.48	53.25	39.36	348.21	25.83	374.04
10	0.46	1.55	53.25	38.26	386.47	25.83	412.30

For example, PV in the second year will be 47.94 million USD, by using $n = 2$. Likewise, the PV of OC needs to be calculated every year.

Computation of Life Cycle Cost

The LCC sheet is prepared as per Table 4.6, by calculating the yearly PV of IC and OC.

Note: For calculating the present value for all the years as per Tables 4.3 and 4.6, a constant discount rate of 8% and an inflation rate of 5% have been considered. However, different forecasted discount rates and inflation rates can be used year on year basis.

ANALYSIS

The Total Cumulative LCC values for every year are plotted in a graph for both the options (refer to Figure 4.1). The graph gives a clear indication of the total LCC of both the options which helps in understanding the most cost-effective solution amongst the options.

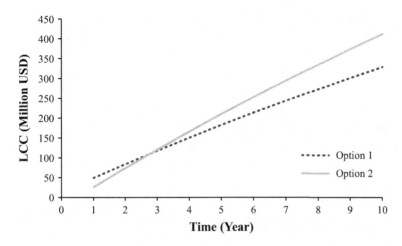

FIGURE 4.1
LCCA for Options 1 and 2

The conclusion from the analysis is as follows:

- The Initial Cost of option 2 (i.e., Semi-automated machines) is lower.
- From third year onward, the LCC for option 1 (i.e., Sophisticated CNC machines) is considerably lower than option 2.

Considering the above Life Cycle Cost Analysis (LCCA), Sophisticated CNC machines (option 1) are preferred compared to Semi-automated machines (option 2).

DISCOUNT RATE AND INFLATION RATE

Forecasting discount rate and inflation rate is hard task and most unpredictable. There are various theories related to forecasting discount rate and inflation rate.

DISCOUNT RATE

The discount rate is used to calculate the present value. The discount rate is the minimal expected return on an investment given its unique risk profile. When estimating the present value of money to be received in the future, the term "discount rate" is used. The term "discount" implies "to subtract an amount." To calculate the present value of money, a discount rate is applied to its future worth. The discount rate shall have implications not only for current investments but also for long-term investments.

There is a fundamental difference between discount rate and interest rate. Discount rates are charged to commercial banks or depository institutions for accepting short-term loans from Federal or Central Reserve Banks. However, interest rates are imposed on loans given to borrowers by lenders. Banks, financial institutions, or people can act as lenders.

As the purpose is to calculate the present value of a future cost discounted in today's time, the current discount rate during the time of LCCA can be used. In LCCA, a year-on-year basis forecasted discount rate may not be required to calculate each year's discount rate.

INFLATION RATE

Inflation is defined as an increase in the overall cost of goods and services in an economy. As the total price level rises, each unit of currency purchases less goods and services; hence, inflation equals a loss of buying power of money.

The Phillips curve is an economic notion that states that unemployment and inflation have a stable and inverse relationship.

The Phillips curve is derived from Equation 4.1.

$$\pi = \pi^e - \beta(u - u_n) + \vartheta \qquad (4.1)$$

Here,

π = inflation.

π^e = the expected inflation.

β = a parameter that measures the response of inflation in relation to cyclical unemployment.

u = unemployment.

u_n = the natural rate of unemployment.

ϑ = supply shocks.

The Phillips curve is named after economist A.W. Phillips. He studied unemployment and wages in the United Kingdom from 1861 to 1957. Phillips discovered an inverse relationship between the rate of wage growth and the level of unemployment. Although the relationship existed in the United States for a period till the 1960s, it was put into doubt by the 1970s stagflation. When an economy faces slow economic growth, high unemployment, and high price inflation, it is referred to as stagflation. This scenario completely contradicts the principle underlying the Phillips curve. Stagflation did not occur in the United States until the 1970s when growing unemployment did not correspond with lowering inflation. After that economic pattern changed and it was not possible to predict inflation by using the Phillips curve directly. To overcome this scenario, a new economic model appeared which is known as the inflation-augmented Phillips curve (refer to Equation 4.2).

$$\pi = \pi^e - h\left(u - u_n\right) \qquad (4.2)$$

Here,

π = inflation.
π^e = the expected inflation.
u = unemployment.
u_n = the natural rate of unemployment.
h = a fixed positive coefficient.

Using Equation 4.2, a forecasted inflation rate can be calculated. That single inflation rate can be used for all the years to evaluate LCCA. On the other hand, the year-wise inflation rate can also be calculated, and different forecasted inflation rates for each year can be used in the spreadsheet provided in Tables 4.3 and 4.6. As an alternative, to avoid the calculation for forecasting inflation, the current year's inflation rate as per available data from reliable source can be used for every year. For example, if today's inflation rate is 5%, then the same can be used as the forecasted inflation rate for coming years for calculating LCCA.

5

Salvage Value

The Life Cycle Cost computation as per Tables 4.3 and 4.6 have not considered salvage value into account. The salvage value is the estimated carrying amount of the asset after depreciation, based on the value the business expects to receive in exchange for the asset at the end of its useful life. The salvage value or residual value of an asset or system is its remaining value at the end of the its life cycle period. Salvage values can be based on resale value, residual value, scrap value, or disposal value.

For LCCA, the salvage value of an entity needs to be calculated for each year. Accordingly, the present value (PV) for the same needs to be calculated on a year-on-year basis. Then this PV of salvage value should be subtracted from the Life Cycle Cost of each year to get the final Life Cycle Cost value of that year. While all other cost elements are getting added in LCCA, salvage value is always subtracted from cost elements. Because salvage value is not a cost element, rather it is the potential earning value of the asset at the end of its life.

For the computation of the Life Cycle Cost of option 1, the salvage value can be introduced in Table 4.3. Table 5.1 demonstrates an LCCA calculation sheet with salvage value for option 1 as per clause 4.1.

By following the above-mentioned concept, Life Cycle Cost can be computed for option 2 as well considering estimated salvage values.

DOI: 10.4324/9781003462330-6

TABLE 5.1

Life Cycle Cost Calculation with Salvage Value for Option 1

	Factors		Operation and Maintenance cost (OC)			PV of Initial Cost (IC)	Salvage Value in nth Year	PV of Salvage Value	Total LCC
Time Period	Discounting Factor	Inflation Factor	Future OC in nth Year	PV of Any Year	Total PV Incurred				
nth Year	$1/(1+8/100)^n$	$(1+5/100)^{(n-1)}$			$F = E +$ last year's F				
			USD	USD	USD	USD	USD	USD	USD
A	B	C	D	$E = D \times B \times C$		G	J	$K = J \times B \times C$	$H = G + F - K$
1	0.93	1	0	0	0	48.98	24.49	22.68	26.30
2	0.86	1.05	38.60	34.75	34.75	48.98	22.04	19.84	63.89
3	0.79	1.10	38.60	33.78	68.53	48.98	19.59	17.15	100.36
4	0.74	1.16	38.60	32.84	101.37	48.98	17.14	14.59	135.77
5	0.68	1.22	38.60	31.93	133.31	48.98	14.69	12.16	170.13
6	0.63	1.28	38.60	31.04	164.35	48.98	12.25	9.85	203.48
7	0.58	1.34	38.60	30.18	194.53	48.98	9.80	7.66	235.86
8	0.54	1.41	38.60	29.34	223.88	48.98	7.35	5.59	267.27
9	0.50	1.48	38.60	28.53	252.41	48.98	4.90	3.62	297.77
10	0.46	1.55	38.60	27.74	280.14	48.98	2.45	1.76	327.37

SHALL SALVAGE VALUE BE REDUCED TO PRESENT VALUE (PV)?

In the example given in Table 5.1, the PV of salvage value for each year has been calculated. However, for accounting purposes, as a notion, salvage value is not reduced to present value. An asset's salvage value is its estimated value after it has been rendered useless for its original use. The assessment would not be accurate if we discounted the salvage value to its present value since the scrap value would be relatively low at that time. For LCCA, it is the discretion of the analyst whether the present value of salvage value is to be calculated or the salvage value can be put straightway without calculating the present value.

The salvage value is simply an estimate. Nobody knows what a piece of property will cost after a particular period. The asset may also wind up in a junkyard.

In Table 5.1, the salvage value for each year was available from some references. However, in general, if salvage value is not provided then it needs to be estimated based on experience or any other available data by using the concept of depreciation. Salvage value can be considered as the depreciated value of an asset.

Equation 5.1 may be used for calculating salvage value in any particular year.

$$S = P\left(1 - i\right)^{n} \tag{5.1}$$

Where,

S = the salvage value in the nth year.
P = the original value of the asset.
i = the depreciation rate.

DEPRECIATION

Depreciation in accounting refers to the real decrease in the value of an asset, such as the decrease in the value of an asset as it is utilized each year. In economics, depreciation is the progressive loss in the market value of any entity over time as a result of physical wear and tear, obsolescence, or changes in demand. Economic depreciation is not always as straightforward as accounting depreciation. Accounting depreciation reduces the value of a tangible asset over time according to a predetermined depreciation plan. Economic depreciation causes a loss in the value of an item that is not necessarily uniform or scheduled but rather is determined by relevant economic forces.

There is an asset-specific depreciation rate guideline as per corporate governance law for many countries. Those rates can be used for calculating the depreciated value of the asset, i.e., salvage value.

Depreciated value can be calculated by using the straight-line method, i.e., SLM (where the loss in asset value is assumed to be the same every year over its lifetime) or written down value, i.e., WDV (where the asset loses more value in the earlier years and less in the later years). For LCCA, the depreciation rate as per WDV may be used in Equation 5.1.

6

Sample Life Cycle Cost Analysis Report

BACKGROUND

The XYZ Urban Planning Council (referred to as the Owner) has proposed to develop the ABC Housing Development – Villa Project (referred to as the Project) which is a residential villa development in MNY city. The proposed project has been planned to be designed as per the Sustainable Green Building Program developed by XYZ Urban Planning Council which would follow a standardized Rating System.

The Sustainable Green Building Program is the initiative which will transform the city into a model of sustainable urbanization. It aims to create a more sustainable society and cities and to develop equilibrium between the three pillars of sustainability (Figure 6.1):

- **Environment**
- **Economy**
- **Social**

In the immediate term, the Sustainable Green Building Program is focused on the rapidly changing built environment. It is making significant improvements to influence projects under design, development, or construction within the city. One of the key initiatives for the Sustainable Green Building Program is the Standardized Rating System.

The Rating System aims to address the sustainability of a given development throughout its lifecycle from concept to operation. The Rating System provides design guidance and detailed requirements for

DOI: 10.4324/9781003462330-7

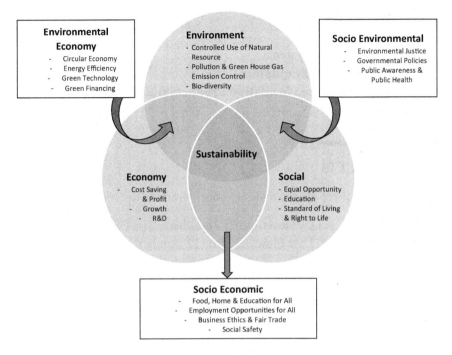

FIGURE 6.1
Sustainability diagram

evaluating a villa's potential performance with the three pillars of the Sustainable Green Building Program.

As per the Rating System, Life Cycle Cost Analysis (LCCA) for villa projects has to be carried out from the concept design stages. The LCC model must be maintained and upgraded throughout the design stages. LCCA intends to enable effective long-term decisions about villa design and construction to maximize efficiency over the whole life of the development.

BUILDING ALTERNATIVES

A thorough LCCA of the alternatives is done before finalizing the various design options and building materials for the project. Options with the logical and effective Life Cycle Cost are taken into the project consideration.

The following building components are analyzed for different alternatives:

- **Water Faucets**
- **Water Closets**
- **Solar Hot Water Systems**
- **Air-Conditioning Equipment**
- **Building Envelope (Insulation Products and Glazing)**
- **Lighting**

WATER FAUCETS

For the project, three alternatives are considered for water faucets:

Option 1: Model 1, Low Flow 6 lpm (12 numbers, Cost USD 200 per faucet)

Option 2: Model 2, Low Flow 5.5 lpm (12 numbers, Cost USD 450 per faucet)

Option 3: Model 3 Faucets 2.5 lpm (12 numbers, Cost USD 1200 per faucet)

TABLE 6.1

Cost Estimate for Water Faucet – Option 1

Model 1, Low Flow 6 lpm (1.6 gpm)			
Initial Cost			
Sl. No.	Cost Element	Value (in USD)/Year	Time Phase	Remarks
---	---	---	---	---
1	Design and development (D)	0.00	–	Bought out item
2	Investment in asset (A)	2400.00	0–1 year	12 numbers, Cost USD 200 per faucet
3	Installation (I)	1000.00	0–1 year	
	Total	3400.00	0–1 year	
Operation and Maintenance Cost			
Sl. No.	Cost Element	Value (in USD)/Year	Time Phase	Remarks
1	Labour (L)	0.00	2–25 years	No labour
2	Energy/Operational/ Utility (E)	3066.00	2–25 years	30 usages per day x 1.6 gallons per min x 30 sec usage x 0.35 USD per gallon x 365 days
3	Spare and maintenance (S)	200.00	2–25 years	Maintenance and repair
4	Raw material (M)	0.00	2–25 years	
	Total	3266.00	2–25 years	

TABLE 6.2

Cost Estimate for Water Faucet – Option 2

Model 2, Low Flow 5.5 lpm (1.45 gpm)				
Initial Cost				
Sl. No.	Cost Element	Value (in USD)/Year	Time Phase	Remarks
1	Design and development (D)	0.00	–	Bought out item
2	Investment in asset (A)	5400.00	0–1 year	12 numbers, Cost USD 450 per faucet
3	Installation (I)	1000.00	0–1 year	
	Total	6400.00	0–1 year	
Operation and Maintenance Cost				
Sl. No.	Cost Element	Value (in USD)/Year	Time Phase	Remarks
1	Labour (L)	0.00	2–25 years	
2	Energy/Operational/ Utility (E)	2778.56	2–25 years	30 usages per day x 1.45 gallons per min x 30 sec usage x 0.35 USD per gallon x 365 days
3	Spare and maintenance (S)	200.00	2–25 years	Maintenance and spare
4	Raw material (M)	0.00	2–25 years	
	Total	2978.56	2–25 years	

Following are the input and output for the LCCA:

Input: Cost Estimate Sheet for Options (consisting of Tables 6.1, 6.2, and 6.3)

Output: LCCA Computation Sheet for Options (consisting of Tables 6.4, 6.5, and 6.6)

Comparison of Life Cycle Costs for the options are plotted in Figure 6.2.

Conclusion

The Initial Cost of option 1 is the lowest. From a life cycle point of view, option 3 is more cost-effective than options 1 and 2. But the Life Cycle

TABLE 6.3

Cost Estimate for Water Faucet – Option 3

Model 3 Faucets 2.5 lpm (.67 gpm)				
Initial Cost				
Sl. No.	Cost Element	Value (in USD)/Year	Time Phase	Remarks
1	Design and development (D)	0.00	–	Bought out item
2	Investment in asset (A)	14400.00	0–1 year	12 numbers, Cost USD 1200 per faucet
3	Installation (I)	1200.00	0–1 year	1% of asset cost
	Total	15600.00	0–1 year	
Operation and Maintenance Cost				
Sl. No.	Cost Element	Value (in USD)/Year	Time Phase	Remarks
1	Labour (L)	0.00	2–25 years	
2	Energy/Operational/ Utility (E)	1283.89	2–25 years	30 usages per day x 0.67 gallons per min x 30 sec usage x 0.35 USD per gallon x 365 days
3	Spare and maintenance (S)	200.00	2–25 years	
4	Raw material (M)	0.00	2–25 years	
	Total	1483.89	2–25 years	

Cost of option 3 crosses the Life Cycle Cost of option 1 in the ninth year, which is very long with regards to the life span of faucets. The Life Cycle Cost of option 3 crosses the Life Cycle Cost of option 2 in the eighth year, which is also very long with regard to the life span of faucets.

On the other hand, the Life Cycle Cost of option 2 crosses the Life Cycle Cost of option 1 in the 17th year, which does not have any practical value considering the life span of a faucet.

Considering the practical approach, option 1 suits the purpose, in the best possible way. Hence, the project design team has decided to go ahead with option 1 (i.e., Model 1, Low Flow 6 lpm).

TABLE 6.4

Life Cycle Costing for Water Faucet – Option 1

			Model 1, Low Flow 6 lpm (1.6 gpm)							
	Factors		Operation and Maintenance Cost (OC)			Initial Cost (IC)				
Time Period	Discounting Factor	Inflation Factor	Future OC in nth Year	Present Value (PV) of Any Year	Total PV Incurred	IC in nth Year	PV of Any Year	Salvage Value at Any Year	PV of Salvage Value	Total LCC
nth Year	$1/(1+8/100)^n$	$(1+5/100)^{(n-1)}$	USD	USD	USD	USD	USD	USD	USD	USD
1	0.93	1	0	0	0	3400.00	3148.15	0.00	0.00	3148.15
2	0.86	1.05	3266.00	2940.07	2940.07	3400.00	3148.15	0.00	0.00	6088.22
3	0.79	1.10	3266.00	2858.40	5798.48	3400.00	3148.15	0.00	0.00	8946.62
4	0.74	1.16	3266.00	2779.00	8577.48	3400.00	3148.15	0.00	0.00	11725.63
5	0.68	1.22	3266.00	2701.81	11279.29	3400.00	3148.15	0.00	0.00	14427.44
6	0.63	1.28	3266.00	2626.76	13906.05	3400.00	3148.15	0.00	0.00	17054.19
7	0.58	1.34	3266.00	2553.79	16459.84	3400.00	3148.15	0.00	0.00	19607.99
8	0.54	1.41	3266.00	2482.85	18942.69	3400.00	3148.15	0.00	0.00	22090.84
9	0.50	1.48	3266.00	2413.89	21356.58	3400.00	3148.15	0.00	0.00	24504.73
10	0.46	1.55	3266.00	2346.83	23703.41	3400.00	3148.15	0.00	0.00	26851.56
11	0.43	1.63	3266.00	2281.64	25985.06	3400.00	3148.15	0.00	0.00	29133.20
12	0.40	1.71	3266.00	2218.26	28203.32	3400.00	3148.15	0.00	0.00	31351.47
13	0.37	1.80	3266.00	2156.65	30359.97	3400.00	3148.15	0.00	0.00	33508.12
14	0.34	1.89	3266.00	2096.74	32456.71	3400.00	3148.15	0.00	0.00	35604.86

(Continued)

TABLE 6.4 (CONTINUED)

Life Cycle Costing for Water Faucet – Option 1

| Time Period | Factors | | Operation and Maintenance Cost (OC) | | | Initial Cost (IC) | | Salvage Value at Any Year | PV of Salvage Value | Total LCC |
| | Discounting Factor | Inflation Factor | Future OC in nth Year | Present Value (PV) of Any Year | Total PV Incurred | IC in nth Year | PV of Any Year | | | |
nth Year	$1/(1+8/100)^n$	$(1+5/100)^{(n-1)}$	USD	USD	USD	USD	USD	USD	USD	USD
15	0.32	1.98	3266.00	2038.50	34495.20	3400.00	3148.15	0.00	0.00	37643.35
16	0.29	2.08	3266.00	1981.87	36477.08	3400.00	3148.15	0.00	0.00	39625.22
17	0.27	2.18	3266.00	1926.82	38403.90	3400.00	3148.15	0.00	0.00	41552.04
18	0.25	2.29	3266.00	1873.30	40277.19	3400.00	3148.15	0.00	0.00	43425.34
19	0.23	2.41	3266.00	1821.26	42098.45	3400.00	3148.15	0.00	0.00	45246.60
20	0.21	2.53	3266.00	1770.67	43869.12	3400.00	3148.15	0.00	0.00	47017.27
21	0.20	2.65	3266.00	1721.49	45590.61	3400.00	3148.15	0.00	0.00	48738.76
22	0.18	2.79	3266.00	1673.67	47264.28	3400.00	3148.15	0.00	0.00	50412.42
23	0.17	2.93	3266.00	1627.18	48891.45	3400.00	3148.15	0.00	0.00	52039.60
24	0.16	3.07	3266.00	1581.98	50473.43	3400.00	3148.15	0.00	0.00	53621.58
25	0.15	3.23	3266.00	1538.03	52011.46	3400.00	3148.15	0.00	0.00	55159.61

Model 1, Low Flow 6 lpm (1.6 gpm)

TABLE 6.5

Life Cycle Costing for Water Faucet – Option 2

<table>
<tr><th colspan="11" align="center">Model 2, Low Flow 5.5 lpm (1.45 gpm)</th></tr>
<tr><th></th><th colspan="2">Factors</th><th colspan="3">Operation and Maintenance Cost (OC)</th><th colspan="2">Initial Cost (IC)</th><th>Salvage Value at a Particular Year</th><th>PV of Salvage Value</th><th>Total LCC</th></tr>
<tr><th>Time Period</th><th>Discounting Factor</th><th>Inflation Factor</th><th>Future OC in nth Year</th><th>PV of Any Year</th><th>Total PV Incurred</th><th>IC in nth Year</th><th>PV of Any Year</th><th></th><th></th><th></th></tr>
<tr><th>nth Year</th><th>$1/(1+8/100)^n$</th><th>$(1+5/100)^{(n-1)}$</th><th>USD</th><th>USD</th><th>USD</th><th>USD</th><th>USD</th><th>USD</th><th>USD</th><th>USD</th></tr>
<tr><td>1</td><td>0.93</td><td>1</td><td>0</td><td>0</td><td>0</td><td>6400.00</td><td>5925.93</td><td>0.00</td><td>0.00</td><td>5925.93</td></tr>
<tr><td>2</td><td>0.86</td><td>1.05</td><td>2978.56</td><td>2681.32</td><td>2681.32</td><td>6400.00</td><td>5925.93</td><td>0.00</td><td>0.00</td><td>8607.25</td></tr>
<tr><td>3</td><td>0.79</td><td>1.10</td><td>2978.56</td><td>2606.84</td><td>5288.16</td><td>6400.00</td><td>5925.93</td><td>0.00</td><td>0.00</td><td>11214.08</td></tr>
<tr><td>4</td><td>0.74</td><td>1.16</td><td>2978.56</td><td>2534.43</td><td>7822.58</td><td>6400.00</td><td>5925.93</td><td>0.00</td><td>0.00</td><td>13748.51</td></tr>
<tr><td>5</td><td>0.68</td><td>1.22</td><td>2978.56</td><td>2464.03</td><td>10286.61</td><td>6400.00</td><td>5925.93</td><td>0.00</td><td>0.00</td><td>16212.53</td></tr>
<tr><td>6</td><td>0.63</td><td>1.28</td><td>2978.56</td><td>2395.58</td><td>12682.19</td><td>6400.00</td><td>5925.93</td><td>0.00</td><td>0.00</td><td>18608.11</td></tr>
<tr><td>7</td><td>0.58</td><td>1.34</td><td>2978.56</td><td>2329.04</td><td>15011.22</td><td>6400.00</td><td>5925.93</td><td>0.00</td><td>0.00</td><td>20937.15</td></tr>
<tr><td>8</td><td>0.54</td><td>1.41</td><td>2978.56</td><td>2264.34</td><td>17275.56</td><td>6400.00</td><td>5925.93</td><td>0.00</td><td>0.00</td><td>23201.49</td></tr>
<tr><td>9</td><td>0.50</td><td>1.48</td><td>2978.56</td><td>2201.44</td><td>19477.01</td><td>6400.00</td><td>5925.93</td><td>0.00</td><td>0.00</td><td>25402.93</td></tr>
<tr><td>10</td><td>0.46</td><td>1.55</td><td>2978.56</td><td>2140.29</td><td>21617.30</td><td>6400.00</td><td>5925.93</td><td>0.00</td><td>0.00</td><td>27543.22</td></tr>
<tr><td>11</td><td>0.43</td><td>1.63</td><td>2978.56</td><td>2080.84</td><td>23698.14</td><td>6400.00</td><td>5925.93</td><td>0.00</td><td>0.00</td><td>29624.06</td></tr>
<tr><td>12</td><td>0.40</td><td>1.71</td><td>2978.56</td><td>2023.04</td><td>25721.17</td><td>6400.00</td><td>5925.93</td><td>0.00</td><td>0.00</td><td>31647.10</td></tr>
<tr><td>13</td><td>0.37</td><td>1.80</td><td>2978.56</td><td>1966.84</td><td>27688.02</td><td>6400.00</td><td>5925.93</td><td>0.00</td><td>0.00</td><td>33613.94</td></tr>
<tr><td>14</td><td>0.34</td><td>1.89</td><td>2978.56</td><td>1912.21</td><td>29600.22</td><td>6400.00</td><td>5925.93</td><td>0.00</td><td>0.00</td><td>35526.15</td></tr>
</table>

(Continued)

TABLE 6.5 (CONTINUED)

Life Cycle Costing for Water Faucet – Option 2

			Model 2, Low Flow 5.5 lpm (1.45 gpm)							
	Factors		Operation and Maintenance Cost (OC)			Initial Cost (IC)		Salvage Value at a Particular Year	PV of Salvage Value	Total LCC
Time Period	Discounting Factor	Inflation Factor	Future OC in nth Year	PV of Any Year	Total PV Incurred	IC in nth Year	PV of Any Year			
nth Year	$1/(1+8/100)^n$	$(1+5/100)^{(n-1)}$	USD	USD	USD	USD	USD	USD	USD	USD
15	0.32	1.98	2978.56	1859.09	31459.31	6400.00	5925.93	0.00	0.00	37385.24
16	0.29	2.08	2978.56	1807.45	33266.76	6400.00	5925.93	0.00	0.00	39192.69
17	0.27	2.18	2978.56	1757.24	35024.01	6400.00	5925.93	0.00	0.00	40949.93
18	0.25	2.29	2978.56	1708.43	36732.44	6400.00	5925.93	0.00	0.00	42658.36
19	0.23	2.41	2978.56	1660.97	38393.41	6400.00	5925.93	0.00	0.00	44319.34
20	0.21	2.53	2978.56	1614.84	40008.25	6400.00	5925.93	0.00	0.00	45934.17
21	0.20	2.65	2978.56	1569.98	41578.22	6400.00	5925.93	0.00	0.00	47504.15
22	0.18	2.79	2978.56	1526.37	43104.59	6400.00	5925.93	0.00	0.00	49030.52
23	0.17	2.93	2978.56	1483.97	44588.56	6400.00	5925.93	0.00	0.00	50514.49
24	0.16	3.07	2978.56	1442.75	46031.31	6400.00	5925.93	0.00	0.00	51957.24
25	0.15	3.23	2978.56	1402.67	47433.98	6400.00	5925.93	0.00	0.00	53359.91

TABLE 6.6

Life Cycle Costing for Water Faucet – Option 3

	Factors		Operation and Maintenance Cost (OC)			Initial Cost (IC)		Salvage Value at Particular Year	PV of Salvage Value	Total LCC
Time Period	Discounting Factor	Inflation Factor	Future OC in nth Year	PV of Any Year	Total PV Incurred	IC in nth Year	PV of Any Year			
nth Year	$1/(1+8/100)^n$	$(1+5/100)^{(n-1)}$	USD	USD	USD	USD	USD	USD	USD	USD
1	0.93	1	0	0	0	15600.00	14444.44	0.00	0.00	14444.44
2	0.86	1.05	1483.89	1335.80	1335.80	15600.00	14444.44	0.00	0.00	15780.25
3	0.79	1.10	1483.89	1298.70	2634.50	15600.00	14444.44	0.00	0.00	17078.95
4	0.74	1.16	1483.89	1262.62	3897.13	15600.00	14444.44	0.00	0.00	18341.57
5	0.68	1.22	1483.89	1227.55	5124.68	15600.00	14444.44	0.00	0.00	19569.12
6	0.63	1.28	1483.89	1193.45	6318.13	15600.00	14444.44	0.00	0.00	20762.57
7	0.58	1.34	1483.89	1160.30	7478.43	15600.00	14444.44	0.00	0.00	21922.87
8	0.54	1.41	1483.89	1128.07	8606.50	15600.00	14444.44	0.00	0.00	23050.94
9	0.50	1.48	1483.89	1096.73	9703.23	15600.00	14444.44	0.00	0.00	24147.68
10	0.46	1.55	1483.89	1066.27	10769.50	15600.00	14444.44	0.00	0.00	25213.95
11	0.43	1.63	1483.89	1036.65	11806.15	15600.00	14444.44	0.00	0.00	26250.60
12	0.40	1.71	1483.89	1007.86	12814.01	15600.00	14444.44	0.00	0.00	27258.45
13	0.37	1.80	1483.89	979.86	13793.87	15600.00	14444.44	0.00	0.00	28238.31
14	0.34	1.89	1483.89	952.64	14746.51	15600.00	14444.44	0.00	0.00	29190.95
15	0.32	1.98	1483.89	926.18	15672.69	15600.00	14444.44	0.00	0.00	30117.13

Model 3 Faucets 2.5 lpm (.67 gpm)

(Continued)

TABLE 6.6 (CONTINUED)

Life Cycle Costing for Water Faucet – Option 3

	Factors		Operation and Maintenance Cost (OC)			Initial Cost (IC)		Salvage Value at Particular Year	PV of Salvage Value	Total LCC
Time Period	Discounting Factor	Inflation Factor	Future OC in nth Year	PV of Any Year	Total PV Incurred	IC in nth Year	PV of Any Year			
nth Year	$1/(1+8/100)^n$	$(1+5/100)^{(n-1)}$	USD	USD	USD	USD	USD	USD	USD	USD
16	0.29	2.08	1483.89	900.45	16573.14	15600.00	14444.44	0.00	0.00	31017.59
17	0.27	2.18	1483.89	875.44	17448.58	15600.00	14444.44	0.00	0.00	31893.02
18	0.25	2.29	1483.89	851.12	18299.70	15600.00	14444.44	0.00	0.00	32744.15
19	0.23	2.41	1483.89	827.48	19127.18	15600.00	14444.44	0.00	0.00	33571.62
20	0.21	2.53	1483.89	804.49	19931.67	15600.00	14444.44	0.00	0.00	34376.12
21	0.20	2.65	1483.89	782.15	20713.82	15600.00	14444.44	0.00	0.00	35158.26
22	0.18	2.79	1483.89	760.42	21474.24	15600.00	14444.44	0.00	0.00	35918.68
23	0.17	2.93	1483.89	739.30	22213.54	15600.00	14444.44	0.00	0.00	36657.98
24	0.16	3.07	1483.89	718.76	22932.30	15600.00	14444.44	0.00	0.00	37376.74
25	0.15	3.23	1483.89	698.80	23631.09	15600.00	14444.44	0.00	0.00	38075.54

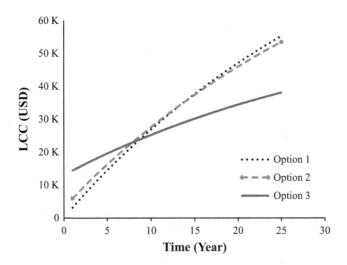

FIGURE 6.2
Comparison of Life Cycle Cost for Faucets

WATER CLOSETS

For the project, three alternatives are considered for water closets:

Option 1: Model 1, Dual Flush 6/4 l/s (6 numbers, Cost USD 1200 per flash)
Option 2: Model 2, Dual Flush 6/3 l/s (6 numbers, Cost USD 1800 per flash)
Option 3: Model 3, Dual Flush 4/2 l/s (6 numbers, Cost USD 3200 per flash)

Following are the input and output for the LCCA:

Input: Cost Estimate Sheet for Options (consisting of Tables 6.7, 6.8, and 6.9)

TABLE 6.7

Cost Estimate for Water Closet – Option 1

	Dual Flush 6/4 l/s			
	Initial Cost			
Sl. No.	**Cost Element**	**Value (in USD)/Year**	**Time Phase**	**Remarks**
1	Design and development (D)	0.00	–	Bought out item
2	Investment in asset (A)	7200.00	0–1 year	6 numbers, Cost USD 1200 per flash
3	Installation (I)	2000.00	0–1 year	
	Total	9200.00	0–1 year	
	Operation and Maintenance Cost			
Sl. No.	**Cost Element**	**Value (in USD)/Year**	**Time Phase**	**Remarks**
1	Labour (L)	0.00	2–25 years	No labour
2	Energy/Operational/Utility (E)	3598.00	2–25 years	Estimated water use
3	Spare and maintenance (S)	200.00	2–25 years	Maintenance and repair
4	Raw material (M)	0.00	2–25 years	
	Total	3798.00	2–25 years	

Output: LCCA Computation Sheet for Options (consisting of Tables 6.10, 6.11, and 6.12)

Comparison of Life Cycle Cost for these options are plotted in Figure 6.3.

TABLE 6.8

Cost Estimate for Water Closet – Option 2

Dual Flush 6/3 l/s			
Initial Cost			
Sl. No.	Cost Element	Value (in USD)/Year	Time Phase	Remarks
1	Design and development (D)	0.00	–	Bought out item
2	Investment in asset (A)	10800.00	0–1 year	6 numbers, Cost USD 1800 per flash
3	Installation (I)	2000.00	0–1 year	
	Total	12800.00	0–1 year	
Operation and Maintenance Cost			
Sl. No.	Cost Element	Value (in USD)/Year	Time Phase	Remarks
1	Labour (L)	0.00	2–25 years	
2	Energy/Operational/Utility (E)	3266.00	2–25 years	Estimated water use
3	Spare and maintenance (S)	200.00	2–25 years	Maintenance and spare
4	Raw material (M)	0.00	2–25 years	
	Total	3466.00	2–25 years	

Conclusion

The Initial Cost of option 1 is the lowest. However, from a life cycle point of view, option 3 is the most cost-effective. The Life Cycle Cost of option 3 crosses the Life Cycle Cost of option 1 in the tenth year, which is a very

TABLE 6.9

Cost Estimate for Water Closet – Option 3

		Dual Flush 4/2 l/s		
		Initial Cost		
Sl. No.	**Cost Element**	**Value (in USD)/Year**	**Time Phase**	**Remarks**
1	Design and development (D)	0.00	–	Bought out item
2	Investment in asset (A)	19200.00	0–1 year	6 numbers, Cost USD 3200 per flash
3	Installation (I)	2000.00	0–1 year	
	Total	21200.00	0–1 year	
		Operation and Maintenance Cost		
Sl. No.	**Cost Element**	**Value (in USD)/Year**	**Time Phase**	**Remarks**
1	Labour (L)	0.00	2–25 years	
2	Energy/Operational/Utility (E)	2193.00	2–25 years	Estimated water use
3	Spare and maintenance (S)	200.00	2–25 years	Maintenance and spare
4	Raw material (M)	0.00	2–25 years	
	Total	2393.00	2–25 years	

long time with regard to the life span of closets. The Life Cycle Cost of option 3 crosses the Life Cycle Cost of option 2 in the tenth year, too, which is also very long with regard to the life span of closets.

On the other hand, the Life Cycle Cost of option 2 crosses the Life Cycle Cost of option 1 in the 15th year, which has not any practical value.

TABLE 6.10

Life Cycle Costing for Water Closet – Option 1

Time		Factors		Dual Flush 6/4 l/s							
				Operation and Maintenance Cost (OC)			Initial Cost (IC)		Salvage Value at a Particular Year	PV of Salvage Value	Total LCC
Time Period	*n*th Year	Discounting Factor	Inflation Factor	Future OC in *n*th Year	PV of Any Year	Total PV Incurred	IC in *n*th Year	PV of any Year			
		$1/(1+8/100)^n$	$(1+5/100)^{(n-1)}$	USD	USD	USD	USD	USD	USD	USD	USD
1		0.93	1	0	0	0	9200.00	8518.52	0.00	0.00	8518.52
2		0.86	1.05	3798.00	3418.98	3418.98	9200.00	8518.52	0.00	0.00	11937.50
3		0.79	1.10	3798.00	3324.01	6742.99	9200.00	8518.52	0.00	0.00	15261.51
4		0.74	1.16	3798.00	3231.68	9974.67	9200.00	8518.52	0.00	0.00	18493.19
5		0.68	1.22	3798.00	3141.91	13116.57	9200.00	8518.52	0.00	0.00	21635.09
6		0.63	1.28	3798.00	3054.63	16171.21	9200.00	8518.52	0.00	0.00	24689.73
7		0.58	1.34	3798.00	2969.78	19140.99	9200.00	8518.52	0.00	0.00	27659.51
8		0.54	1.41	3798.00	2887.29	22028.28	9200.00	8518.52	0.00	0.00	30546.79
9		0.50	1.48	3798.00	2807.08	24835.36	9200.00	8518.52	0.00	0.00	33353.88
10		0.46	1.55	3798.00	2729.11	27564.47	9200.00	8518.52	0.00	0.00	36082.99
11		0.43	1.63	3798.00	2653.30	30217.77	9200.00	8518.52	0.00	0.00	38736.29
12		0.40	1.71	3798.00	2579.60	32797.37	9200.00	8518.52	0.00	0.00	41315.89
13		0.37	1.80	3798.00	2507.94	35305.31	9200.00	8518.52	0.00	0.00	43823.83
14		0.34	1.89	3798.00	2438.28	37743.59	9200.00	8518.52	0.00	0.00	46262.11
15		0.32	1.98	3798.00	2370.55	40114.14	9200.00	8518.52	0.00	0.00	48632.66

TABLE 6.10 (CONTINUED)

Life Cycle Costing for Water Closet – Option 1

Time	Factors		Dual Flush 6/4 l/s Operation and Maintenance Cost (OC)			Initial Cost (IC)		Salvage Value at a Particular Year	PV of Salvage Value	Total LCC
Time Period	Discounting Factor	Inflation Factor	Future OC in nth Year	PV of Any Year	Total PV Incurred	IC in nth Year	PV of any Year			
nth Year	$1/(1+8/100)^n$	$(1+5/100)^{(n-1)}$	USD	USD	USD	USD	USD	USD	USD	USD
16	0.29	2.08	3798.00	2304.70	42418.84	9200.00	8518.52	0.00	0.00	50937.36
17	0.27	2.18	3798.00	2240.68	44659.52	9200.00	8518.52	0.00	0.00	53178.04
18	0.25	2.29	3798.00	2178.44	46837.96	9200.00	8518.52	0.00	0.00	55356.48
19	0.23	2.41	3798.00	2117.93	48955.89	9200.00	8518.52	0.00	0.00	57474.41
20	0.21	2.53	3798.00	2059.10	51014.98	9200.00	8518.52	0.00	0.00	59533.50
21	0.20	2.65	3798.00	2001.90	53016.88	9200.00	8518.52	0.00	0.00	61535.40
22	0.18	2.79	3798.00	1946.29	54963.17	9200.00	8518.52	0.00	0.00	63481.69
23	0.17	2.93	3798.00	1892.23	56855.40	9200.00	8518.52	0.00	0.00	65373.92
24	0.16	3.07	3798.00	1839.66	58695.06	9200.00	8518.52	0.00	0.00	67213.58
25	0.15	3.23	3798.00	1788.56	60483.63	9200.00	8518.52	0.00	0.00	69002.15

TABLE 6.11

Life Cycle Costing for Water Closet – Option 2

Time		Factors		Operation and Maintenance Cost (OC)			Initial Cost (IC)		Salvage Value at a Particular Year	PV of Salvage Value	Total LCC
				Dual Flush 6/3 l/s							
Time Period		Discounting Factor	Inflation Factor	Future OC in nth Year	PV of Any Year	Total PV Incurred	IC in nth Year	PV of Any Year			
nth Year		$1/(1+8/100)^n$	$(1+5/100)^{(n-1)}$	USD	USD	USD	USD	USD	USD	USD	USD
1		0.93	1	0	0	0	12800.00	11851.85	0.00	0.00	11851.85
2		0.86	1.05	3466.00	3120.11	3120.11	12800.00	11851.85	0.00	0.00	14971.97
3		0.79	1.10	3466.00	3033.44	6153.56	12800.00	11851.85	0.00	0.00	18005.41
4		0.74	1.16	3466.00	2949.18	9102.74	12800.00	11851.85	0.00	0.00	20954.59
5		0.68	1.22	3466.00	2867.26	11970.00	12800.00	11851.85	0.00	0.00	23821.85
6		0.63	1.28	3466.00	2787.61	14757.61	12800.00	11851.85	0.00	0.00	26609.46
7		0.58	1.34	3466.00	2710.18	17467.79	12800.00	11851.85	0.00	0.00	29319.64
8		0.54	1.41	3466.00	2634.90	20102.69	12800.00	11851.85	0.00	0.00	31954.54
9		0.50	1.48	3466.00	2561.71	22664.39	12800.00	11851.85	0.00	0.00	34516.24
10		0.46	1.55	3466.00	2490.55	25154.94	12800.00	11851.85	0.00	0.00	37006.79
11		0.43	1.63	3466.00	2421.36	27576.30	12800.00	11851.85	0.00	0.00	39428.16
12		0.40	1.71	3466.00	2354.10	29930.41	12800.00	11851.85	0.00	0.00	41782.26
13		0.37	1.80	3466.00	2288.71	32219.12	12800.00	11851.85	0.00	0.00	44070.97

(Continued)

TABLE 6.11 (CONTINUED)

Life Cycle Costing for Water Closet – Option 2

					Dual Flush 6/3 l/s								
Time		Factors			Operation and Maintenance Cost (OC)				Initial Cost (IC)				
												Salvage Value at a	PV of
Time Period	Discounting Factor	Inflation Factor		Future OC in nth Year	PV of Any Year	Total PV Incurred		IC in nth Year	PV of Any Year		Particular Year	Salvage Value	Total LCC
nth Year	$1/(1+8/100)^n$	$(1+5/100)^{(n-1)}$	USD	USD	USD	USD		USD	USD		USD	USD	USD
14	0.34	1.89	3466.00	2225.14	34444.26		12800.00	11851.85		0.00		0.00	46296.11
15	0.32	1.98	3466.00	2163.33	36607.59		12800.00	11851.85		0.00		0.00	48459.44
16	0.29	2.08	3466.00	2103.24	38710.82		12800.00	11851.85		0.00		0.00	50562.67
17	0.27	2.18	3466.00	2044.81	40755.64		12800.00	11851.85		0.00		0.00	52607.49
18	0.25	2.29	3466.00	1988.01	42743.65		12800.00	11851.85		0.00		0.00	54595.50
19	0.23	2.41	3466.00	1932.79	44676.44		12800.00	11851.85		0.00		0.00	56528.29
20	0.21	2.53	3466.00	1879.10	46555.54		12800.00	11851.85		0.00		0.00	58407.39
21	0.20	2.65	3466.00	1826.90	48382.44		12800.00	11851.85		0.00		0.00	60234.29
22	0.18	2.79	3466.00	1776.16	50158.60		12800.00	11851.85		0.00		0.00	62010.45
23	0.17	2.93	3466.00	1726.82	51885.42		12800.00	11851.85		0.00		0.00	63737.27
24	0.16	3.07	3466.00	1678.85	53564.27		12800.00	11851.85		0.00		0.00	65416.12
25	0.15	3.23	3466.00	1632.22	55196.49		12800.00	11851.85		0.00		0.00	67048.34

TABLE 6.12

Life Cycle Costing for Water Closet – Option 3

			Dual Flush 4/2 l/s							
Time	**Factors**		**Operation and Maintenance Cost (OC)**			**Initial Cost (IC)**				
Time Period	**Discounting Factor**	**Inflation Factor**	**Future OC in nth Year**	**PV of Any Year**	**Total PV Incurred**	**IC in nth Year**	**PV of Any Year**	**Salvage Value at a Particular Year**	**PV of Salvage Value**	**Total LCC**
nth Year	$1/(1+8/100)^n$	$(1+5/100)^{(n-1)}$	USD	USD	USD	USD	USD	USD	USD	USD
1	0.93	1	0	0	0	21200.00	19629.63	0.00	0.00	19629.63
2	0.86	1.05	2393.00	2154.19	2154.19	21200.00	19629.63	0.00	0.00	21783.82
3	0.79	1.10	2393.00	2094.35	4248.55	21200.00	19629.63	0.00	0.00	23878.18
4	0.74	1.16	2393.00	2036.18	6284.72	21200.00	19629.63	0.00	0.00	25914.35
5	0.68	1.22	2393.00	1979.62	8264.34	21200.00	19629.63	0.00	0.00	27893.97
6	0.63	1.28	2393.00	1924.63	10188.97	21200.00	19629.63	0.00	0.00	29818.60
7	0.58	1.34	2393.00	1871.17	12060.13	21200.00	19629.63	0.00	0.00	31689.76
8	0.54	1.41	2393.00	1819.19	13879.32	21200.00	19629.63	0.00	0.00	33508.95
9	0.50	1.48	2393.00	1768.66	15647.98	21200.00	19629.63	0.00	0.00	35277.61
10	0.46	1.55	2393.00	1719.53	17367.50	21200.00	19629.63	0.00	0.00	36997.13
11	0.43	1.63	2393.00	1671.76	19039.27	21200.00	19629.63	0.00	0.00	38668.90
12	0.40	1.71	2393.00	1625.32	20664.59	21200.00	19629.63	0.00	0.00	40294.22
13	0.37	1.80	2393.00	1580.18	22244.77	21200.00	19629.63	0.00	0.00	41874.39

TABLE 6.12 (CONTINUED)

Life Cycle Costing for Water Closet – Option 3

Dual Flush 4/2 l/s

| Time Period | Factors | | Operation and Maintenance Cost (OC) | | | Initial Cost (IC) | | Salvage Value at a Particular Year | PV of Salvage Value | Total LCC |
| | Discounting Factor | Inflation Factor | Future OC in nth Year | PV of Any Year | Total PV Incurred | IC in nth Year | PV of Any Year | | | |
nth Year	$1/(1+8/100)^n$	$(1+5/100)^{(n-1)}$	USD	USD	USD	USD	USD	USD	USD	USD
14	0.34	1.89	2393.00	1536.28	23781.05	21200.00	19629.63	0.00	0.00	43410.68
15	0.32	1.98	2393.00	1493.61	25274.66	21200.00	19629.63	0.00	0.00	44904.28
16	0.29	2.08	2393.00	1452.12	26726.77	21200.00	19629.63	0.00	0.00	46356.40
17	0.27	2.18	2393.00	1411.78	28138.56	21200.00	19629.63	0.00	0.00	47768.19
18	0.25	2.29	2393.00	1372.57	29511.12	21200.00	19629.63	0.00	0.00	49140.75
19	0.23	2.41	2393.00	1334.44	30845.56	21200.00	19629.63	0.00	0.00	50475.19
20	0.21	2.53	2393.00	1297.37	32142.93	21200.00	19629.63	0.00	0.00	51772.56
21	0.20	2.65	2393.00	1261.33	33404.27	21200.00	19629.63	0.00	0.00	53033.89
22	0.18	2.79	2393.00	1226.30	34630.56	21200.00	19629.63	0.00	0.00	54260.19
23	0.17	2.93	2393.00	1192.23	35822.79	21200.00	19629.63	0.00	0.00	55452.42
24	0.16	3.07	2393.00	1159.11	36981.91	21200.00	19629.63	0.00	0.00	56611.54
25	0.15	3.23	2393.00	1126.92	38108.83	21200.00	19629.63	0.00	0.00	57738.46

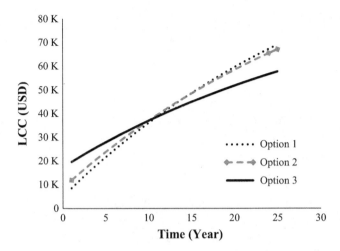

FIGURE 6.3
Comparison of Life Cycle Cost for Closets

Considering the practical approach, option 1 suits the purpose, in the best possible way. Hence, the project design team has decided to go ahead with option 1 (i.e., Dual Flush 6/4 l/s).

SOLAR HOT WATER SYSTEMS

Solar hot water systems use a collector to absorb heat from the sun and transfer that heat to water, which is stored for use as needed.

Solar water heaters are one of the most important parts of green building requirements. In the first option, 50% of the hot water requirements for the villa are served by solar water heaters while in the second alternative, all of the hot water requirements will be supplied by solar water heaters.

Two alternatives for solar hot water systems are considered for the project:

Option 1: Solar Water Heater – 100% (All of the hot water requirements will be supplied by solar water heaters which can potentially save a considerable electrical power.)

TABLE 6.13

Cost Estimate for Solar Water Heater – 100% – Option 1

	Solar Water Heater – 100%			
	Initial Cost			
Sl. No.	Cost Element	Value (in USD)/Year	Time Phase	Remarks
1	Design and development (D)	0.00	-	Bought out item
2	Investment in asset (A)	32000.00	0–1 year	
3	Installation (I)	7500.00	0–1 year	
	Total	39500.00	0–1 year	
	Operation and Maintenance Cost			
Sl. No.	Cost Element	Value (in USD)/Year	Time Phase	Remarks
1	Labour (L)	0.00	2–25 years	No labour
2	Energy (E)	0.00	2–25 years	No electrical energy consumed
3	Spare and maintenance (S)	800.00	2–25 years	
4	Raw material (M)	0.00	2–25 years	
	Total	800.00	2–25 years	

Option 2: Solar Water Heater – 50% (50% of the hot water requirements will be supplied by solar water heaters. The other 50% is served by conventional electrical heater sources.)

Following are the input and output for the LCCA:

Input: Cost Estimate Sheet for Options (consisting of Tables 6.13 and 6.14)

Output: LCCA Computation Sheet for Options (consisting of Tables 6.15 and 6.16)

Comparison of Life Cycle Cost for these options are plotted in Figure 6.4.

TABLE 6.14

Cost Estimate for Solar Water Heater – 50% – Option 2

Solar Water Heater – 50%				
Initial Cost				
Sl. No.	Cost Element	Value (in USD)/Year	Time Phase	Remarks
1	Design and development (D)	0.00	-	Bought out item
2	Investment in asset (A)	24000.00	0–1 year	
3	Installation (I)	4000.00	0–1 year	
	Total	28000.00	0–1 year	
Operation and Maintenance Cost				
Sl. No.	Cost Element	Value (in USD)/Year	Time Phase	Remarks
1	Labour (L)	0.00	2–25 years	
2	Energy (E)	2400.00	2–25 years	50% water heated by electrical heater. Energy cost of electrical heater in a year.
3	Spare and maintenance (S)	500.00	2–25 years	
4	Raw material (M)	0.00	2–25 years	
	Total	2900.00	2–25 years	

Conclusion

Although the initial investment is higher in option 1, however considering a study period of 25 years, the overall Life Cycle Cost for option 1 becomes more effective than option 2 from the sixth year onwards.

Considering the practical approach, option 1 (Solar Water Heater – 100%) suits the purpose. Hence, the project design team has decided to go ahead with option 1 (Solar Water Heater – 100%).

TABLE 6.15

Life Cycle Costing for Solar Water Heater – 100% – Option 1

Time			Factors		Operation and Maintenance Cost (OC)			Initial Cost (IC)		Salvage Value at a Particular Year	PV of Salvage Value	Total LCC
Time Period		nth Year	Discounting Factor	Inflation Factor	Future OC in nth Year	PV of Any Year	Total PV Incurred	IC in nth Year	PV of Any Year			
			$1/(1+8/100)^n$	$(1+5/100)^{(n-1)}$	USD	USD	USD	USD	USD	USD	USD	USD
1			0.93	1	0	0	0	39500.00	36574.07	11850.00	10972.22	25601.85
2			0.86	1.05	800.00	720.16	720.16	39500.00	36574.07	11455.00	10311.86	26982.38
3			0.79	1.10	800.00	700.16	1420.32	39500.00	36574.07	11060.00	9679.71	28314.69
4			0.74	1.16	800.00	680.71	2101.04	39500.00	36574.07	10665.00	9074.73	29600.38
5			0.68	1.22	800.00	661.80	2762.84	39500.00	36574.07	10270.00	8495.89	30841.02
6			0.63	1.28	800.00	643.42	3406.26	39500.00	36574.07	9875.00	7942.20	32038.13
7			0.58	1.34	800.00	625.55	4031.80	39500.00	36574.07	9480.00	7412.72	33193.15
8			0.54	1.41	800.00	608.17	4639.97	39500.00	36574.07	9085.00	6906.53	34307.52
9			0.50	1.48	800.00	591.28	5231.25	39500.00	36574.07	8690.00	6422.74	35382.58
10			0.46	1.55	800.00	574.85	5806.10	39500.00	36574.07	8295.00	5960.50	36419.68
11			0.43	1.63	800.00	558.88	6364.99	39500.00	36574.07	7900.00	5518.98	37420.08
12			0.40	1.71	800.00	543.36	6908.35	39500.00	36574.07	7505.00	5097.39	38385.03
13			0.37	1.80	800.00	528.27	7436.61	39500.00	36574.07	7110.00	4694.97	39315.72
14			0.34	1.89	800.00	513.59	7950.20	39500.00	36574.07	6715.00	4310.96	40213.31

(Continued)

TABLE 6.15 (CONTINUED)

Life Cycle Costing for Solar Water Heater – 100% – Option 1

	Factors		Operation and Maintenance Cost (OC)			Initial Cost (IC)		Salvage Value at a Particular Year	PV of Salvage Value	Total LCC
Time Period	Discounting Factor	Inflation Factor	Future OC in nth Year	PV of Any Year	Total PV Incurred	IC in nth Year	PV of Any Year			
nth Year	$1/(1+8/100)^n$	$(1+5/100)^{(n-1)}$	USD	USD	USD	USD	USD	USD	USD	USD
15	0.32	1.98	800.00	499.33	8449.53	39500.00	36574.07	6320.00	3944.67	41078.93
16	0.29	2.08	800.00	485.46	8934.99	39500.00	36574.07	5925.00	3595.40	41913.65
17	0.27	2.18	800.00	471.97	9406.96	39500.00	36574.07	5530.00	3262.50	42718.53
18	0.25	2.29	800.00	458.86	9865.82	39500.00	36574.07	5135.00	2945.31	43494.58
19	0.23	2.41	800.00	446.11	10311.93	39500.00	36574.07	4740.00	2643.23	44242.78
20	0.21	2.53	800.00	433.72	10745.65	39500.00	36574.07	4345.00	2355.65	44964.07
21	0.20	2.65	800.00	421.67	11167.33	39500.00	36574.07	3950.00	2082.02	45659.38
22	0.18	2.79	800.00	409.96	11577.29	39500.00	36574.07	3555.00	1821.76	46329.60
23	0.17	2.93	800.00	398.57	11975.86	39500.00	36574.07	3160.00	1574.36	46975.57
24	0.16	3.07	800.00	387.50	12363.36	39500.00	36574.07	2765.00	1339.30	47598.13
25	0.15	3.23	800.00	376.74	12740.10	39500.00	36574.07	2370.00	1116.09	48198.09

TABLE 6.16

Life Cycle Costing for Solar Water Heater – 50% – Option 2

Time		Factors		Operation and Maintenance Cost (OC)			Initial Cost (IC)		Salvage Value at a Particular Year	PV of Salvage Value	Total LCC
Time Period		Discounting Factor	Inflation Factor	Future OC in nth Year	PV of Any Year	Total PV Incurred	IC in nth Year	PV of Any Year			
nth Year		$1/(1+8/100)^n$	$(1+5/100)^{(n-1)}$	USD	USD	USD	USD	USD	USD	USD	USD
1		0.93	1	0	0	0	28000.00	25925.93	8400.00	7777.78	18148.15
2		0.86	1.05	2900.00	2610.60	2610.60	28000.00	25925.93	8120.00	7309.67	21226.85
3		0.79	1.10	2900.00	2538.08	5148.68	28000.00	25925.93	7840.00	6861.57	24213.03
4		0.74	1.16	2900.00	2467.58	7616.25	28000.00	25925.93	7560.00	6432.72	27109.46
5		0.68	1.22	2900.00	2399.03	10015.29	28000.00	25925.93	7280.00	6022.40	29918.81
6		0.63	1.28	2900.00	2332.39	12347.68	28000.00	25925.93	7000.00	5629.92	32643.69
7		0.58	1.34	2900.00	2267.61	14615.29	28000.00	25925.93	6720.00	5254.59	35286.63
8		0.54	1.41	2900.00	2204.62	16819.91	28000.00	25925.93	6440.00	4895.77	37850.06
9		0.50	1.48	2900.00	2143.38	18963.28	28000.00	25925.93	6160.00	4552.83	40336.38
10		0.46	1.55	2900.00	2083.84	21047.12	28000.00	25925.93	5880.00	4225.16	42747.88
11		0.43	1.63	2900.00	2025.95	23073.08	28000.00	25925.93	5600.00	3912.19	45086.81
12		0.40	1.71	2900.00	1969.68	25042.75	28000.00	25925.93	5320.00	3613.34	47355.34
13		0.37	1.80	2900.00	1914.96	26957.72	28000.00	25925.93	5040.00	3328.08	49555.57
14		0.34	1.89	2900.00	1861.77	28819.49	28000.00	25925.93	4760.00	3055.87	51689.54
15		0.32	1.98	2900.00	1810.06	30629.54	28000.00	25925.93	4480.00	2796.22	53759.25

(Continued)

TABLE 6.16 (CONTINUED)

Life Cycle Costing for Solar Water Heater – 50% – Option 2

Time	Factors		Operation and Maintenance Cost (OC)			Initial Cost (IC)		Salvage Value at a Particular Year	PV of Salvage Value	Total LCC
Time Period	Discounting Factor	Inflation Factor	Future OC in nth Year	PV of Any Year	Total PV Incurred	IC in nth Year	PV of Any Year			
nth Year	$1/(1+8/100)^n$	$(1+5/100)^{(n-1)}$	USD	USD	USD	USD	USD	USD	USD	USD
16	0.29	2.08	2900.00	1759.78	32389.32	28000.00	25925.93	4200.00	2548.64	55766.61
17	0.27	2.18	2900.00	1710.89	34100.21	28000.00	25925.93	3920.00	2312.66	57713.48
18	0.25	2.29	2900.00	1663.37	35763.58	28000.00	25925.93	3640.00	2087.81	59601.69
19	0.23	2.41	2900.00	1617.16	37380.75	28000.00	25925.93	3360.00	1873.68	61432.99
20	0.21	2.53	2900.00	1572.24	38952.99	28000.00	25925.93	3080.00	1669.83	63209.08
21	0.20	2.65	2900.00	1528.57	40481.56	28000.00	25925.93	2800.00	1475.86	64931.62
22	0.18	2.79	2900.00	1486.11	41967.67	28000.00	25925.93	2520.00	1291.38	66602.22
23	0.17	2.93	2900.00	1444.83	43412.50	28000.00	25925.93	2240.00	1116.01	68222.42
24	0.16	3.07	2900.00	1404.69	44817.19	28000.00	25925.93	1960.00	949.38	69793.74
25	0.15	3.23	2900.00	1365.67	46182.86	28000.00	25925.93	1680.00	791.15	71317.64

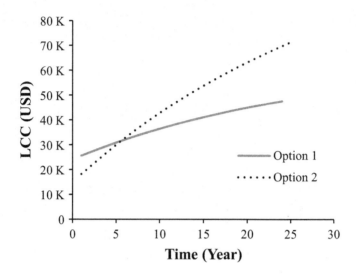

FIGURE 6.4
Comparison of Life Cycle Cost for Solar Hot Water System

AIR-CONDITIONING EQUIPMENT

Cooling and air-conditioning of buildings in hot areas accounts for a huge electricity consumption in the summer months and is the major consumer of electricity. The use of high-performance air-conditioning equipment can result in considerable energy, emissions, and cost savings. Proper air-conditioning equipment can reduce the overall demand for electricity and greenhouse gas emissions.

Three alternatives for air-conditioning equipment have been considered for the project:

Option 1: Model 1 – Variable Refrigerant Flow 410a
Option 2: Model 2 – Conventional System R 410a
Option 3: Model 3 – Conventional System R 410a – Energy Efficient

Following are the input and output for the LCCA:

Input: Cost Estimate Sheet for Options (consisting of Tables 6.17, 6.18, and 6.19)

TABLE 6.17

Cost Estimate for Air Conditioner Model 1, Variable Refrigerant Flow 410a – Option 1

Model 1 – Variable Refrigerant Flow 410a				
Initial Cost				
Sl. No.	Cost Element	Value (in USD)/Year	Time Phase	Remarks
1	Design and development (D)	0.00	-	Bought out item
2	Investment in asset (A)	75617.00	0–1 year	
3	Installation (I)	6250.00	0–1 year	
	Total	81867.00	0–1 year	
Operation and Maintenance Cost				
Sl. No.	Cost Element	Value (in USD)/Year	Time Phase	Remarks
1	Labour (L)	0.00	2–25 years	No labour
2	Energy/Operational (E)	102203.64	2–25 years	
3	Spare and maintenance (S)	500.00	2–25 years	Maintenance and repair
4	Raw material (M)	0.00	2–25 years	
	Total	102703.64	2–25 years	

TABLE 6.18

Cost Estimate for Air Conditioner Model 2, Conventional System R 410a – Option 2

Model 2 – Conventional system R 410a				
Initial Cost				
Sl. No.	Cost Element	Value (in USD)/Year	Time Phase	Remarks
1	Design and development (D)	0.00	-	Bought out item
2	Investment in asset (A)	58570.00	0–1 year	
3	Installation (I)	14407.00	0–1 year	
	Total	72977.00	0–1 year	
Operation and Maintenance Cost				
Sl. No.	Cost Element	Value (in USD)/Year	Time Phase	Remarks
1	Labour (L)	0.00	2–25 years	
2	Energy/Operational (E)	102203.64	2–25 years	
3	Spare and maintenance (S)	800.00	2–25 years	Maintenance and spare
4	Raw material (M)	0.00	2–25 years	
	Total	103003.64	2–25 years	

TABLE 6.19

Cost Estimate for Air Conditioner Model 3, Conventional System R 410a, Energy Efficient – Option 3

	Model 3 – Conventional System R 410a, Energy Efficient			
	Initial Cost			
Sl. No.	**Cost Element**	**Value (in USD)/ Year**	**Time Phase**	**Remarks**
1	Design and development (D)	0.00	–	Bought out item
2	Investment in asset (A)	64870.00	0–1 year	
3	Installation (I)	12600.00	0–1 year	
	Total	77470.00	0–1 year	
	Operation and Maintenance Cost			
Sl. No.	**Cost Element**	**Value (in USD)/ Year**	**Time Phase**	**Remarks**
1	Labour (L)	0.00	2–25 years	
2	Energy/Operational (E)	58402.08	2–25 years	
3	Spare and maintenance (S)	1200.00	2–25 years	
4	Raw material (M)	0.00	2–25 years	
	Total	59602.08	2–25 years	

Output: LCCA Computation Sheet for Options (consisting of Tables 6.20, 6.21, and 6.22)

Comparison of Life Cycle Cost for these options is plotted in Figure 6.5.

TABLE 6.20

Life Cycle Costing for Air Conditioner – Model 1, Variable Refrigerant Flow 410a – Option 1

Time	Factors		Operation and Maintenance Cost (OC)			Initial Cost (IC)					
Time Period	Discounting Factor	Inflation Factor	Future OC in nth Year	PV of Any Year	Total PV Incurred	IC in nth Year	PV of Any Year	Salvage Value at a Particular Year	PV of Salvage Value	Total LCC
nth Year	$1/(1+8/100)^n$	$(1+5/100)^{(n-1)}$	USD	USD	USD	USD	USD	USD	USD	USD
1	0.93	1	0	0	0	81867.00	75802.78	24560.10	22740.83	53061.94
2	0.86	1.05	102703.64	92454.41	92454.41	81867.00	75802.78	23741.43	21372.17	146885.01
3	0.79	1.10	102703.64	89886.23	182340.64	81867.00	75802.78	22922.76	20062.00	238081.42
4	0.74	1.16	102703.64	87389.39	269730.03	81867.00	75802.78	22104.09	18808.13	326724.68
5	0.68	1.22	102703.64	84961.91	354691.94	81867.00	75802.78	21285.42	17608.43	412886.28
6	0.63	1.28	102703.64	82601.85	437293.79	81867.00	75802.78	20466.75	16460.87	496635.70
7	0.58	1.34	102703.64	80307.36	517601.15	81867.00	75802.78	19648.08	15363.48	578040.45
8	0.54	1.41	102703.64	78076.60	595677.75	81867.00	75802.78	18829.41	14314.35	657166.17
9	0.50	1.48	102703.64	75907.80	671585.55	81867.00	75802.78	18010.74	13311.66	734076.67
10	0.46	1.55	102703.64	73799.25	745384.81	81867.00	75802.78	17192.07	12353.62	808833.96
11	0.43	1.63	102703.64	71749.27	817134.08	81867.00	75802.78	16373.40	11438.54	881498.32
12	0.40	1.71	102703.64	69756.24	886890.32	81867.00	75802.78	15554.73	10564.76	952128.34
13	0.37	1.80	102703.64	67818.57	954708.89	81867.00	75802.78	14736.06	9730.70	1020780.96
14	0.34	1.89	102703.64	65934.72	1020643.61	81867.00	75802.78	13917.39	8934.83	1087511.56

(*Continued*)

TABLE 6.20 (CONTINUED)

Life Cycle Costing for Air Conditioner – Model 1, Variable Refrigerant Flow 410a – Option 1

Time	Factors		Model 1 – Variable Refrigerant Flow 410a							
			Operation and Maintenance Cost (OC)			Initial Cost (IC)		Salvage Value at a Particular Year	PV of Salvage Value	Total LCC
Time Period	Discounting Factor	Inflation Factor	Future OC in nth Year	PV of Any Year	Total PV Incurred	IC in nth Year	PV of Any Year			
nth Year	$1/(1+8/100)^n$	$(1+5/100)^{(n-1)}$	USD	USD	USD	USD	USD	USD	USD	USD
15	0.32	1.98	102703.64	64103.20	1084746.80	81867.00	75802.78	13098.72	8175.66	1152373.92
16	0.29	2.08	102703.64	62322.55	1147069.36	81867.00	75802.78	12280.05	7451.77	1215420.36
17	0.27	2.18	102703.64	60591.37	1207660.73	81867.00	75802.78	11461.38	6761.79	1276701.71
18	0.25	2.29	102703.64	58908.28	1266569.00	81867.00	75802.78	10642.71	6104.40	1336267.38
19	0.23	2.41	102703.64	57271.94	1323840.94	81867.00	75802.78	9824.04	5478.30	1394165.41
20	0.21	2.53	102703.64	55681.05	1379521.99	81867.00	75802.78	9005.37	4882.29	1450442.48
21	0.20	2.65	102703.64	54134.35	1433656.34	81867.00	75802.78	8186.70	4315.15	1505143.97
22	0.18	2.79	102703.64	52630.62	1486286.96	81867.00	75802.78	7368.03	3775.76	1558313.98
23	0.17	2.93	102703.64	51168.66	1537455.62	81867.00	75802.78	6549.36	3263.00	1609995.40
24	0.16	3.07	102703.64	49747.31	1587202.93	81867.00	75802.78	5730.69	2775.82	1660229.89
25	0.15	3.23	102703.64	48365.44	1635568.37	81867.00	75802.78	4912.02	2313.18	1709057.97

TABLE 6.21

Life Cycle Costing for Air Conditioner – Model 2, Conventional System R 410a – Option 2

Time	**Factors**		**Model 2 – Conventional System R 410a**										
			Operation and Maintenance Cost (OC)			**Initial Cost (IC)**			**Salvage Value at a Particular Year**	**PV of Salvage Value**	**Total LCC**		
Time Period	**Discounting Factor**	**Inflation Factor**	**Future OC in nth Year**	**PV of Any Year**	**Total PV Incurred**	**IC in nth Year**	**PV of Any Year**						
nth Year	$1/(1+8/100)^n$	$(1+5/100)^{(n-1)}$	USD	USD	USD	USD	USD	USD	USD	USD	USD		
1	0.93	1	0	0	0	72977.00	67571.30	21893.10	20271.39	47299.91			
2	0.86	1.05	103003.64	92724.47	92724.47	72977.00	67571.30	21163.33	19051.35	141244.41			
3	0.79	1.10	103003.64	90148.79	182873.26	72977.00	67571.30	20433.56	17883.45	232561.10			
4	0.74	1.16	103003.64	87644.66	270517.92	72977.00	67571.30	19703.79	16765.74	321323.48			
5	0.68	1.22	103003.64	85210.08	355728.00	72977.00	67571.30	18974.02	15696.32	407602.98			
6	0.63	1.28	103003.64	82843.14	438571.14	72977.00	67571.30	18244.25	14673.37	491469.06			
7	0.58	1.34	103003.64	80541.94	519113.08	72977.00	67571.30	17514.48	13695.15	572989.22			
8	0.54	1.41	103003.64	78304.66	597417.74	72977.00	67571.30	16784.71	12759.95	652229.09			
9	0.50	1.48	103003.64	76129.53	673547.27	72977.00	67571.30	16054.94	11866.13	729252.43			
10	0.46	1.55	103003.64	74014.82	747562.10	72977.00	67571.30	15325.17	11012.13	804121.26			
11	0.43	1.63	103003.64	71958.86	819520.95	72977.00	67571.30	14595.40	10196.42	876895.83			
12	0.40	1.71	103003.64	69960.00	889480.95	72977.00	67571.30	13865.63	9417.53	947634.72			
13	0.37	1.80	103003.64	68016.67	957497.62	72977.00	67571.30	13135.86	8674.04	1016394.88			
14	0.34	1.89	103003.64	66127.31	1023624.93	72977.00	67571.30	12406.09	7964.59	1083231.64			

(*Continued*)

TABLE 6.21 (CONTINUED)

Life Cycle Costing for Air Conditioner – Model 2, Conventional System R 410a – Option 2

	Factors		Operation and Maintenance Cost (OC)			Initial Cost (IC)		Salvage		
Time										**Model 2 – Conventional System R 410a**
Time Period	Discounting Factor	Inflation Factor	Future OC in nth Year	PV of Any Year	Total PV Incurred	IC in nth Year	PV of Any Year	Salvage Value at a Particular Year	PV of Salvage Value	Total LCC
nth Year	$1/(1+8/100)^n$	$(1+5/100)^{(n-1)}$	USD	USD	USD	USD	USD	USD	USD	USD
15	0.32	1.98	103003.64	64290.44	1087915.38	72977.00	67571.30	11676.32	7287.86	1148198.82
16	0.29	2.08	103003.64	62504.60	1150419.97	72977.00	67571.30	10946.55	6642.58	1211348.69
17	0.27	2.18	103003.64	60768.36	1211188.33	72977.00	67571.30	10216.78	6027.52	1272732.11
18	0.25	2.29	103003.64	59080.35	1270268.68	72977.00	67571.30	9487.01	5441.52	1332398.47
19	0.23	2.41	103003.64	57439.23	1327707.91	72977.00	67571.30	8757.24	4883.41	1390395.80
20	0.21	2.53	103003.64	55843.69	1383551.61	72977.00	67571.30	8027.47	4352.11	1446770.79
21	0.20	2.65	103003.64	54292.48	1437844.09	72977.00	67571.30	7297.70	3846.57	1501568.82
22	0.18	2.79	103003.64	52784.36	1490628.45	72977.00	67571.30	6567.93	3365.74	1554834.00
23	0.17	2.93	103003.64	51318.12	1541946.57	72977.00	67571.30	5838.16	2908.67	1606609.20
24	0.16	3.07	103003.64	49892.62	1591839.19	72977.00	67571.30	5108.39	2474.39	1656936.10
25	0.15	3.23	103003.64	48506.71	1640345.91	72977.00	67571.30	4378.62	2061.99	1705855.21

TABLE 6.22

Life Cycle Costing for Air Conditioner – Model 3, Conventional System R 410a, Energy Efficient – Option 3

			Model 3 – Conventional system R 410a – Energy Efficient							
Time	**Factors**		**Operation and Maintenance Cost (OC)**			**Initial Cost (IC)**		**Salvage Value at a Particular Year**	**PV of Salvage Value**	**Total LCC**
Time Period	**Discounting Factor**	**Inflation Factor**	**Future OC in nth Year**	**PV of Any Year**	**Total PV Incurred**	**IC in nth Year**	**PV of Any Year**			
nth Year	$1/(1+8/100)^n$	$(1+5/100)^{(n-1)}$	USD	USD	USD	USD	USD	USD	USD	USD
1	0.93	1	0	0	0	77470.00	71731.48	23241.00	21519.44	50212.04
2	0.86	1.05	59602.08	53654.14	53654.14	77470.00	71731.48	22466.30	20224.29	105161.32
3	0.79	1.10	59602.08	52163.74	105817.88	77470.00	71731.48	21691.60	18984.49	158564.87
4	0.74	1.16	59602.08	50714.75	156532.63	77470.00	71731.48	20916.90	17797.96	210466.15
5	0.68	1.22	59602.08	49306.01	205838.64	77470.00	71731.48	20142.20	16662.70	260907.42
6	0.63	1.28	59602.08	47936.40	253775.03	77470.00	71731.48	19367.50	15576.77	309929.74
7	0.58	1.34	59602.08	46604.83	300379.86	77470.00	71731.48	18592.80	14538.32	357573.02
8	0.54	1.41	59602.08	45310.25	345690.11	77470.00	71731.48	17818.10	13545.54	403876.05
9	0.50	1.48	59602.08	44051.63	389741.75	77470.00	71731.48	17043.40	12596.70	448876.53
10	0.46	1.55	59602.08	42827.98	432569.72	77470.00	71731.48	16268.70	11690.12	492611.08
11	0.43	1.63	59602.08	41638.31	474208.03	77470.00	71731.48	15494.00	10824.19	535115.33
12	0.40	1.71	59602.08	40481.69	514689.72	77470.00	71731.48	14719.30	9997.34	576423.87
13	0.37	1.80	59602.08	39357.20	554046.92	77470.00	71731.48	13944.60	9208.07	616570.33
14	0.34	1.89	59602.08	38263.94	592310.86	77470.00	71731.48	13169.90	8454.95	655587.40

(Continued)

TABLE 6.22 (CONTINUED)

Life Cycle Costing for Air Conditioner – Model 3, Conventional System R 410a, Energy Efficient – Option 3

Time	Factors		Model 3 – Conventional system R 410a – Energy Efficient							
			Operation and Maintenance Cost (OC)			Initial Cost (IC)				
Time Period	Discounting Factor	Inflation Factor	Future OC in nth Year	PV of Any Year	Total PV Incurred	IC in nth Year	PV of Any Year	Salvage Value at a Particular Year	PV of Salvage Value	Total LCC
nth Year	$1/(1+8/100)^n$	$(1+5/100)^{(n-1)}$	USD	USD	USD	USD	USD	USD	USD	USD
15	0.32	1.98	59602.08	37201.06	629511.92	77470.00	71731.48	12395.20	7736.55	693506.85
16	0.29	2.08	59602.08	36167.69	665679.61	77470.00	71731.48	11620.50	7051.54	730359.55
17	0.27	2.18	59602.08	35163.04	700842.65	77470.00	71731.48	10845.80	6398.62	766175.51
18	0.25	2.29	59602.08	34186.28	735028.93	77470.00	71731.48	10071.10	5776.53	800983.88
19	0.23	2.41	59602.08	33236.67	768265.60	77470.00	71731.48	9296.40	5184.07	834813.01
20	0.21	2.53	59602.08	32313.42	800579.02	77470.00	71731.48	8521.70	4620.06	867690.44
21	0.20	2.65	59602.08	31415.83	831994.85	77470.00	71731.48	7747.00	4083.39	899642.95
22	0.18	2.79	59602.08	30543.17	862538.02	77470.00	71731.48	6972.30	3572.96	930696.54
23	0.17	2.93	59602.08	29694.75	892232.77	77470.00	71731.48	6197.60	3087.75	960876.50
24	0.16	3.07	59602.08	28869.89	921102.66	77470.00	71731.48	5422.90	2626.73	990207.41
25	0.15	3.23	59602.08	28067.95	949170.61	77470.00	71731.48	4648.20	2188.94	1018713.15

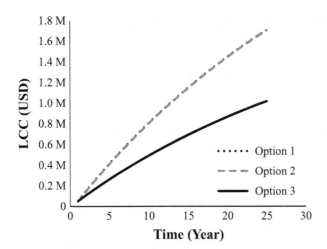

FIGURE 6.5
Comparison of Life Cycle Cost for Air-Conditioning Equipment

Conclusion

The initial costs for all the options are almost similar. Also, Life Cycle Cost of Options 1 and 2 are in almost the same trajectory. Considering Life Cycle Cost, option 3 is the most cost-effective, because of its economic operating cost. Hence, the project design team has decided to go ahead with option 3.

BUILDING ENVELOPE (INSULATION PRODUCTS AND GLAZING)

Selecting the optimum insulation products and systems (i.e., building envelope) is one of the most important factors in ensuring thermal comfort and contributing to energy savings. This study calculated the cooling costs, construction, and Life Cycle Costs for the villa project with different envelope alternatives created by changing the type and thickness of the body and insulation materials used in the walls, floor and roof, which are the structural components forming the building envelope.

Another important part of the building envelope is glazing. Glass and glazing selection play a key role in determining the overall building's thermal performance. The thermal performance of insulating glazing depends mainly on the solar energy transmittance through the glazing and the reflectance of the glazing.

Envelope alternatives with equivalent costs were determined and evaluated.

Rigorous combinations of the building envelope (which includes wall insulation, floor, roof, and glazing) are evaluated, with the best three alternatives mentioned considering their Thermal Transmittance Value (U Value):

Option 1: U Value – Wall 0.316 W/m2/K, Floor 0.148 W/m2/K, and Roof 0.133 W/m2/K

Option 2: U Value – Wall 0.0.320 W/m2/K, Floor 0.148 W/m2/K, and Roof 0.140 W/m2/K

Option 3: U Value – Wall 0.319 W/m2/K, Floor 0.148 W/m2/K, and Roof 0.140 W/m2/K

THERMAL TRANSMITTANCE VALUE (U VALUE)

The capacity of a substance to conduct heat under steady-state circumstances is known as thermal transmittance (U Value). It is a measurement of the amount of heat that will move across a unit area in a unit of time for every unit of temperature differential between the various environments where the substance is present.

Following are the input and output for the LCCA:

Input: Cost Estimate Sheet for Options (consisting of Tables 6.23, 6.24, and 6.25)

TABLE 6.23

Cost Estimate for Building Envelope – Option 1

Building Envelope with the Following Specification:				
U Value: Wall 0.316 W/m2/K, Floor 0.148 W/m2/K, and Roof 0.133 W/m2/K				
Initial Cost				
Sl. No.	**Cost Element**	**Value (in USD)/Year**	**Time Phase**	**Remarks**
1	Design and development (D)	0.00	–	Bought out item
2	Investment in asset (A)	354180.00	0–1 year	
3	Installation (I)	35418.00	0–1 year	
	Total	389598.00	0–1 year	
Operation and Maintenance Cost				
Sl. No.	**Cost Element**	**Value (in USD)/Year**	**Time Phase**	**Remarks**
1	Labour (L)	0.00	2–25 years	No labour
2	Energy/Operational (E)	15050.00	2–25 years	
3	Spare and maintenance (S)	8854.50	2–25 years	Maintenance and repair
4	Raw material (M)	0.00	2–25 years	
	Total	23904.50	2–25 years	

Output: LCCA Computation Sheet for Options (consisting of Tables 6.26, 6.27, and 6.28)

Comparison of Life Cycle Cost for these options are plotted in Figure 6.6.

TABLE 6.24

Cost Estimate for Building Envelope – Option 2

Building Envelope with the Following Specification:			
U Value: Wall 0.0.320 W/m2/K, Floor 0.148 W/m2/K, and Roof 0.140 W/m2/K			
Initial Cost			
Sl. No.	Cost Element	Value (in USD)/ Year	Time Phase	Remarks
---	---	---	---	---
1	Design and development (D)	0.00	–	Bought out item
2	Investment in asset (A)	323516.20	0–1 year	
3	Installation (I)	124646.98	0–1 year	
	Total	448163.18	0–1 year	

Operation and Maintenance Cost			
Sl. No.	Cost Element	Value (in USD)/ Year	Time Phase	Remarks
---	---	---	---	---
1	Labour (L)	0.00	2–25 years	No labour
2	Energy/Operational (E)	19050.63	2–25 years	
3	Spare and maintenance (S)	8087.91	2–25 years	Maintenance and repair
4	Raw material (M)	0.00	2–25 years	
	Total	27138.54	2–25 years	

Conclusion

Out of the three alternatives, Option 1 was selected for the project taking into account the overall lowest Life Cycle Cost.

TABLE 6.25

Cost Estimate for Building Envelope – Option 3

Building Envelope with the Following Specification:			
U Value: Wall 0.319 W/m2/K, Floor 0.148 W/m2/K, and 0.140 W/m2/K			

Initial Cost			
Sl. No.	Cost Element	Value (in USD)/Year	Time Phase	Remarks
---	---	---	---	---
1	Design and development (D)	0.00	–	Bought out item
2	Investment in asset (A)	345106.60	0–1 year	
3	Installation (I)	34510.66	0–1 year	
	Total	379617.26	0–1 year	

Operation and Maintenance Cost			
Sl. No.	Cost Element	Value (in USD)/Year	Time Phase	Remarks
---	---	---	---	---
1	Labour (L)	0.00	2–25 years	No labour
2	Energy/Operational (E)	17363.29	2–25 years	
3	Spare and maintenance (S)	8627.67	2–25 years	Maintenance and repair
4	Raw material (M)	0.00	2–25 years	
	Total	25990.96	2–25 years	

LIGHTING

Lighting is one of the vital components of energy consumption that contributes to the operational cost of a building. It is highly recommended to install energy-efficient lighting fixtures that not only have lesser wattage than conventional fixtures but also have a longer lifetime.

TABLE 6.26

Life Cycle Costing for Building Envelope – Option 1

			Building Envelope with U Value: Wall 0.316 W/m2/K, Floor 0.148 W/m2/K, and Roof 0.133 W/m2/K							
Time	**Factors**		**Operation and Maintenance Cost (OC)**				**Initial Cost (IC)**			
Time Period	**Discounting Factor**	**Inflation Factor**	**Future OC in nth Year**	**PV of Any Year**	**Total PV Incurred**	**IC in nth Year**	**PV of Any Year**	**Salvage Value at a Particular Year**	**PV of Salvage Value**	**Total LCC**
nth Year	$1/(1+8/100)^n$	$(1+5/100)^{(n-1)}$	USD	USD	USD	USD	USD	USD	USD	USD
1	0.93	1	0	0	0	389598.00	360738.89	116879.40	108221.67	252517.22
2	0.86	1.05	23904.50	21518.97	21518.97	389598.00	360738.89	112983.42	101708.33	280549.53
3	0.79	1.10	23904.50	20921.22	42440.19	389598.00	360738.89	109087.44	95473.33	307705.74
4	0.74	1.16	23904.50	20340.07	62780.26	389598.00	360738.89	105191.46	89506.25	334012.90
5	0.68	1.22	23904.50	19775.07	82555.34	389598.00	360738.89	101295.48	83797.00	359497.22
6	0.63	1.28	23904.50	19225.76	101781.10	389598.00	360738.89	97399.50	78335.87	384184.12
7	0.58	1.34	23904.50	18691.72	120472.82	389598.00	360738.89	93503.52	73113.48	408098.22
8	0.54	1.41	23904.50	18172.50	138645.32	389598.00	360738.89	89607.54	68120.78	431263.43
9	0.50	1.48	23904.50	17667.71	156313.03	389598.00	360738.89	85711.56	63349.03	453702.88
10	0.46	1.55	23904.50	17176.94	173489.97	389598.00	360738.89	81815.58	58789.82	475439.03
11	0.43	1.63	23904.50	16699.80	190189.77	389598.00	360738.89	77919.60	54435.02	496493.64
12	0.40	1.71	23904.50	16235.92	206425.69	389598.00	360738.89	74023.62	50276.79	516887.79
13	0.37	1.80	23904.50	15784.92	222210.61	389598.00	360738.89	70127.64	46307.57	536641.93
14	0.34	1.89	23904.50	15346.45	237557.06	389598.00	360738.89	66231.66	42520.07	555775.88
15	0.32	1.98	23904.50	14920.16	252477.22	389598.00	360738.89	62335.68	38907.25	574308.86

(Continued)

TABLE 6.26 (CONTINUED)

Life Cycle Costing for Building Envelope – Option 1

			Building Envelope with U Value: Wall 0.316 W/m2/K, Floor 0.148 W/m2/K, and Roof 0.133 W/m2/K							
Time	Factors		Operation and Maintenance Cost (OC)			Initial Cost (IC)		Salvage Value at a Particular Year	PV of Salvage Value	Total LCC
Time Period	Discounting Factor	Inflation Factor	Future OC in nth Year	PV of Any Year	Total PV Incurred	IC in nth Year	PV of Any Year			
nth Year	$1/(1+8/100)^n$	$(1+5/100)^{(n-1)}$	USD	USD	USD	USD	USD	USD	USD	USD
16	0.29	2.08	23904.50	14505.71	266982.94	389598.00	360738.89	58439.70	35462.34	592259.49
17	0.27	2.18	23904.50	14102.78	281085.71	389598.00	360738.89	54543.72	32178.79	609645.81
18	0.25	2.29	23904.50	13711.03	294796.74	389598.00	360738.89	50647.74	29050.30	626485.34
19	0.23	2.41	23904.50	13330.17	308126.91	389598.00	360738.89	46751.76	26070.78	642795.03
20	0.21	2.53	23904.50	12959.89	321086.80	389598.00	360738.89	42855.78	23234.37	658591.32
21	0.20	2.65	23904.50	12599.89	333686.69	389598.00	360738.89	38959.80	20535.43	673890.15
22	0.18	2.79	23904.50	12249.89	345936.59	389598.00	360738.89	35063.82	17968.50	688706.97
23	0.17	2.93	23904.50	11909.62	357846.21	389598.00	360738.89	31167.84	15528.34	703056.76
24	0.16	3.07	23904.50	11578.80	369425.00	389598.00	360738.89	27271.86	13209.87	716954.02
25	0.15	3.23	23904.50	11257.16	380682.17	389598.00	360738.89	23375.88	11008.22	730412.83

TABLE 6.27

Life Cycle Costing for Building Envelope – Option 2

	Factors		Operation and Maintenance Cost (OC)			Initial Cost (IC)		Salvage Value at a Particular Year	PV of Salvage Value	Total LCC
Time			**Building Envelope with U Value: Wall 0.0.320 W/m2/K, Floor 0.148 W/m2/K, and Roof 0.140 W/m2/K**							
Time Period	Discounting Factor	Inflation Factor	Future OC in nth Year	PV of Any Year	Total PV Incurred	IC in nth Year	PV of Any Year			
nth Year	$1/(1+8/100)^n$	$(1+5/100)^{(n-1)}$	USD	USD	USD	USD	USD	USD	USD	USD
1	0.93	1	0	0	0	448163.18	414965.91	134448.95	124489.77	290476.14
2	0.86	1.05	27138.54	24430.27	24430.27	448163.18	414965.91	129967.32	116997.33	322398.84
3	0.79	1.10	27138.54	23751.65	48181.92	448163.18	414965.91	125485.69	109825.08	353322.74
4	0.74	1.16	27138.54	23091.88	71273.80	448163.18	414965.91	121004.06	102961.01	383278.69
5	0.68	1.22	27138.54	22450.44	93724.24	448163.18	414965.91	116522.43	96393.54	412296.60
6	0.63	1.28	27138.54	21826.82	115551.06	448163.18	414965.91	112040.80	90111.48	440405.48
7	0.58	1.34	27138.54	21220.52	136771.57	448163.18	414965.91	107559.16	84104.05	467633.43
8	0.54	1.41	27138.54	20631.06	157402.63	448163.18	414965.91	103077.53	78360.84	494007.70
9	0.50	1.48	27138.54	20057.97	177460.60	448163.18	414965.91	98595.90	72871.79	519554.72
10	0.46	1.55	27138.54	19500.81	196961.41	448163.18	414965.91	94114.27	67627.23	544300.09
11	0.43	1.63	27138.54	18959.12	215920.53	448163.18	414965.91	89632.64	62617.81	566268.63
12	0.40	1.71	27138.54	18432.48	234353.00	448163.18	414965.91	85151.00	57834.50	591484.41
13	0.37	1.80	27138.54	17920.46	252273.47	448163.18	414965.91	80669.37	53268.62	613970.75
14	0.34	1.89	27138.54	17422.67	269696.14	448163.18	414965.91	76187.74	48911.77	635750.27
15	0.32	1.98	27138.54	16938.71	286634.85	448163.18	414965.91	71706.11	44755.87	656844.88

(Continued)

TABLE 6.27 (CONTINUED)

Life Cycle Costing for Building Envelope – Option 2

Time	Factors			Operation and Maintenance Cost (OC)				Initial Cost (IC)			Salvage Value at a Particular Year	PV of Salvage Value	Total LCC
				Building Envelope with U Value: Wall 0.0.320 W/m2/K, Floor 0.148 W/m2/K, and Roof 0.140 W/m2/K									
Time Period	Discounting Factor	Inflation Factor		Future OC in nth Year	PV of Any Year	Total PV Incurred		IC in nth Year	PV of Any Year				
nth Year	$1/(1+8/100)^n$	$(1+5/100)^{(n-1)}$	USD	USD	USD	USD		USD	USD	USD	USD	USD	USD
16	0.29	2.08	27138.54	16468.19	303103.04		448163.18	414965.91		67224.48	40793.11	677275.83
17	0.27	2.18	27138.54	16010.74	319113.78		448163.18	414965.91		62742.85	37015.97	697063.71
18	0.25	2.29	27138.54	15566.00	334679.77		448163.18	414965.91		58261.21	33417.20	716228.48
19	0.23	2.41	27138.54	15133.61	349813.38		448163.18	414965.91		53779.58	29989.79	734789.50
20	0.21	2.53	27138.54	14713.23	364526.61		448163.18	414965.91		49297.95	26727.01	752765.50
21	0.20	2.65	27138.54	14304.53	378831.14		448163.18	414965.91		44816.32	23622.36	770174.69
22	0.18	2.79	27138.54	13907.18	392738.32		448163.18	414965.91		40334.69	20669.57	787034.66
23	0.17	2.93	27138.54	13520.87	406259.19		448163.18	414965.91		35853.05	17862.59	803362.51
24	0.16	3.07	27138.54	13145.29	419404.48		448163.18	414965.91		31371.42	15195.60	819174.79
25	0.15	3.23	27138.54	12780.14	432184.63		448163.18	414965.91		26889.79	12663.00	834487.53

TABLE 6.28

Life Cycle Costing for Building Envelope – Option 3

			Building Envelope with U Value: Wall 0.319 W/m2/K, Floor 0.148 W/m2/K, and 0.140 W/m2/K							
Time	Factors		Operation and Maintenance Cost (OC)			Initial Cost (IC)		Salvage Value at a Particular Year	PV of Salvage Value	Total LCC
Time Period	Discounting Factor	Inflation Factor	Future OC in nth Year	PV of Any Year	Total PV Incurred	IC at nth Year	PV of Any Year			
nth Year	$1/(1+8/100)^n$	$(1+5/100)^{(n-1)}$	USD	USD	USD	USD	USD	USD	USD	USD
1	0.93	1	0	0	0	379617.26	351497.46	113885.18	105449.24	246048.22
2	0.86	1.05	25990.96	23397.21	23397.21	379617.26	351497.46	110089.01	99102.76	275791.91
3	0.79	1.10	25990.96	22747.29	46144.49	379617.26	351497.46	106292.83	93027.49	304614.47
4	0.74	1.16	25990.96	22115.42	68259.91	379617.26	351497.46	102496.66	87213.27	332544.10
5	0.68	1.22	25990.96	21501.10	89761.01	379617.26	351497.46	98700.49	81650.29	359608.19
6	0.63	1.28	25990.96	20903.85	110664.86	379617.26	351497.46	94904.32	76329.06	385833.26
7	0.58	1.34	25990.96	20323.18	130988.04	379617.26	351497.46	91108.14	71240.46	411245.05
8	0.54	1.41	25990.96	19758.65	150746.69	379617.26	351497.46	87311.97	66375.66	435868.50
9	0.50	1.48	25990.96	19209.80	169956.49	379617.26	351497.46	83515.80	61726.15	459727.80
10	0.46	1.55	25990.96	18676.19	188632.69	379617.26	351497.46	79719.62	57283.74	482846.41
11	0.43	1.63	25990.96	18157.41	206790.10	379617.26	351497.46	75923.45	53040.50	505247.06
12	0.40	1.71	25990.96	17653.04	224443.14	379617.26	351497.46	72127.28	48988.80	526951.81
13	0.37	1.80	25990.96	17162.68	241605.82	379617.26	351497.46	68331.11	45121.26	547982.02
14	0.34	1.89	25990.96	16685.94	258291.75	379617.26	351497.46	64534.93	41430.79	568358.43

(Continued)

TABLE 6.28 (CONTINUED)

Life Cycle Costing for Building Envelope – Option 3

Building Envelope with U Value: Wall 0.319 W/m2/K, Floor 0.148 W/m2/K, and 0.140 W/m2/K

Time	Factors		Operation and Maintenance Cost (OC)			Initial Cost (IC)		Salvage Value at a Particular Year	PV of Salvage Value	Total LCC
Time Period	Discounting Factor	Inflation Factor	Future OC in nth Year	PV of Any Year	Total PV Incurred	IC at nth Year	PV of Any Year			
nth Year	$1/(1+8/100)^n$	$(1+5/100)^{(n-1)}$	USD	USD	USD	USD	USD	USD	USD	USD
15	0.32	1.98	25990.96	16222.44	274514.19	379617.26	351497.46	60738.76	37910.52	588101.13
16	0.29	2.08	25990.96	15771.81	290286.00	379617.26	351497.46	56942.59	34553.86	607229.60
17	0.27	2.18	25990.96	15333.71	305619.71	379617.26	351497.46	53146.42	31354.43	625762.74
18	0.25	2.29	25990.96	14907.77	320527.48	379617.26	351497.46	49350.24	28306.08	643718.86
19	0.23	2.41	25990.96	14493.67	335021.15	379617.26	351497.46	45554.07	25402.90	661115.72
20	0.21	2.53	25990.96	14091.07	349112.22	379617.26	351497.46	41757.90	22639.15	677970.53
21	0.20	2.65	25990.96	13699.65	362811.86	379617.26	351497.46	37961.73	20009.35	694299.97
22	0.18	2.79	25990.96	13319.10	376130.97	379617.26	351497.46	34165.55	17508.18	710120.24
23	0.17	2.93	25990.96	12949.13	389080.09	379617.26	351497.46	30369.38	15130.53	725447.02
24	0.16	3.07	25990.96	12589.43	401669.52	379617.26	351497.46	26573.21	12871.46	740295.52
25	0.15	3.23	25990.96	12239.72	413909.24	379617.26	351497.46	22777.04	10726.21	754680.49

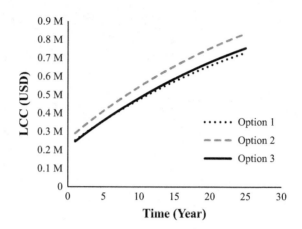

FIGURE 6.6
Comparison of Life Cycle Cost for Building Envelope

Both light-emitting diode (LED) and compact fluorescent lamp (CFL) technologies offer energy-efficient alternatives to inefficient lighting technology such as incandescent bulbs. Depending upon the activities pursued at the different zones of the building appropriate lighting fixtures have been proposed.

A thorough comparison was undertaken to suffice the LCCA for lighting fixtures. Two options were evaluated where option 1 is comprised of fluorescent lamps in all places. In the alternatives a different combination of lamps which includes fluorescent/CFL as well are considered in the design.

TABLE 6.29

Cost Estimate for Lighting – Option 1

	Fluorescent Lamps in All Places			
	Initial Cost			
Sl. No.	**Cost Element**	**Value (in USD)/ Year**	**Time Phase**	**Remarks**
1	Design and development (D)	0.00	–	Bought out item
2	Investment in asset (A)	20000.00	0–1 year	8000 (light fixtures)+ 12000 (electric wiring)
3	Installation (I)	500.00	0–1 year	
	Total	20500.00	0–1 year	
	Operation and Maintenance Cost			
Sl. No.	**Cost Element**	**Value (in USD)/ Year**	**Time Phase**	**Remarks**
1	Labour (L)	0.00	2–25 years	No labour
2	Energy/Operation (E)	3600.00	2–25 years	
3	Spare and maintenance (S)	500.00	2–25 years	
4	Raw material (M)	0.00	2–25 years	
	Total	4100.00	2–25 years	

Two alternative solutions are considered for lighting:

Option 1: Fluorescent lamps in all places
Option 2: Combination of lamps at different places

Following are the input and output for the LCCA:

Input: Cost Estimate Sheet for Options (consisting of Tables 6.29 and 6.30)

TABLE 6.30

Cost Estimate for Lighting – Option 2

		Alternative Lighting Design Case for Villa Project		
		Initial Cost		
Sl. No.	**Cost Element**	**Value (in USD)/Year**	**Time Phase**	**Remarks**
1	Design and development (D)	0.00	–	Bought out item
2	Investment in asset (A)	14700.00	0–1 year	13500 (light fixtures) + 12000 (electric wiring)
3	Installation (I)	500.00	0–1 year	
	Total	15200.00	0–1 year	
		Operation and Maintenance Cost		
Sl. No.	**Cost Element**	**Value (in USD)/Year**	**Time Phase**	**Remarks**
1	Labour (L)	0.00	2–25 years	
2	Energy (E)	1450.00	2–25 years	
3	Spare and maintenance (S)	1200.00	2–25 years	
4	Raw material (M)	0.00	2–25 years	
	Total	2650.00	2–25 years	

Output: LCCA Computation Sheet for Options (consisting of Tables 6.31 and 6.32)

Comparison of Life Cycle Cost for these options are plotted in Figure 6.7.

TABLE 6.31

Life Cycle Costing for Lighting – Option 1

	Fluorescent Lamps in All Places									
	Factors		Operation and Maintenance Cost (OC)			Initial Cost (IC)					
Time	Discounting Factor	Inflation Factor	Future OC in nth Year	PV of Any Year	Total PV Incurred	IC in nth Year	PV of Any Year	Salvage Value at a Particular Year	PV of Salvage Value	Total LCC
Time Period										
nth Year	$1/(1+8/100)^n$	$(1+5/100)^{(n-1)}$	USD	USD	USD	USD	USD	USD	USD	USD
A	B	C	D	$E = D \times B \times C$	$F = E +$ last Year's F	G	H	I	$J = I \times B \times C$	$K = H + F - J$
1	0.93	1	0	0	0	20500.00	18981.48	6150.00	5694.44	13287.04
2	0.86	1.05	4100.00	3690.84	3690.84	20500.00	18981.48	5945.00	5351.72	17320.60
3	0.79	1.10	4100.00	3588.32	7279.16	20500.00	18981.48	5740.00	5023.65	21237.00
4	0.74	1.16	4100.00	3488.64	10767.81	20500.00	18981.48	5535.00	4709.67	25039.62
5	0.68	1.22	4100.00	3391.74	14159.55	20500.00	18981.48	5330.00	4409.26	28731.77
6	0.63	1.28	4100.00	3297.52	17457.07	20500.00	18981.48	5125.00	4121.90	32316.65
7	0.58	1.34	4100.00	3205.93	20662.99	20500.00	18981.48	4920.00	3847.11	35797.37
8	0.54	1.41	4100.00	3116.87	23779.87	20500.00	18981.48	4715.00	3584.40	39176.94
9	0.50	1.48	4100.00	3030.29	26810.16	20500.00	18981.48	4510.00	3333.32	42458.32
10	0.46	1.55	4100.00	2946.12	29756.27	20500.00	18981.48	4305.00	3093.42	45644.33
11	0.43	1.63	4100.00	2864.28	32620.56	20500.00	18981.48	4100.00	2864.28	48737.76

(*Continued*)

TABLE 6.31 (CONTINUED)

Life Cycle Costing for Lighting – Option 1

	Time	Factors		Operation and Maintenance Cost (OC)			Initial Cost (IC)		Salvage Value at a Particular Year	PV of Salvage Value	Total LCC
	Time Period	Discounting Factor	Inflation Factor	Future OC in nth Year	PV of Any Year	Total PV Incurred	IC in nth Year	PV of Any Year			
	nth Year	$1/(1+8/100)^n$	$(1+5/100)^{(n-1)}$	USD	USD	USD	USD	USD	USD	USD	USD
	12	0.40	1.71	4100.00	2784.72	35405.27	20500.00	18981.48	3895.00	2645.48	51741.27
	13	0.37	1.80	4100.00	2707.36	38112.64	20500.00	18981.48	3690.00	2436.63	54657.49
	14	0.34	1.89	4100.00	2632.16	40744.80	20500.00	18981.48	3485.00	2237.34	57488.94
	15	0.32	1.98	4100.00	2559.04	43303.84	20500.00	18981.48	3280.00	2047.24	60238.09
	16	0.29	2.08	4100.00	2487.96	45791.80	20500.00	18981.48	3075.00	1865.97	62907.31
	17	0.27	2.18	4100.00	2418.85	48210.65	20500.00	18981.48	2870.00	1693.19	65498.93
	18	0.25	2.29	4100.00	2351.66	50562.31	20500.00	18981.48	2665.00	1528.58	68015.21
	19	0.23	2.41	4100.00	2286.34	52848.64	20500.00	18981.48	2460.00	1371.80	70458.32
	20	0.21	2.53	4100.00	2222.83	55071.47	20500.00	18981.48	2255.00	1222.55	72830.39
	21	0.20	2.65	4100.00	2161.08	57232.55	20500.00	18981.48	2050.00	1080.54	75133.49
	22	0.18	2.79	4100.00	2101.05	59333.60	20500.00	18981.48	1845.00	945.47	77369.61
	23	0.17	2.93	4100.00	2042.69	61376.29	20500.00	18981.48	1640.00	817.08	79540.69
	24	0.16	3.07	4100.00	1985.95	63362.23	20500.00	18981.48	1435.00	695.08	81648.63
	25	0.15	3.23	4100.00	1930.78	65293.02	20500.00	18981.48	1230.00	579.23	83695.26

TABLE 6.32

Life Cycle Costing for Lighting – Option 2

	Time		Factors		Operation and Maintenance Cost (OC)			Initial Cost (IC)		Salvage Value at a Particular Year	PV of Salvage Value	Total LCC
	Time Period		Discounting Factor	Inflation Factor	Future OC in nth Year	PV of Any Year	Total PV Incurred	IC in nth Year	PV of Any Year			
	nth Year		$1/(1+8/100)^{n}$	$(1+5/100)^{(n-1)}$	USD	USD	USD	USD	USD	USD	USD	USD
	A		B	C	D	$E = D \times B \times C$	$F = E + \text{last year's } F$	G	H	I	$J = I \times B \times C$	$K = H + F - J$
	1		0.93	1	0	0	0	15200.00	14074.07	4560.00	4222.22	9851.85
	2		0.86	1.05	2650.00	2385.55	2385.55	15200.00	14074.07	4408.00	3968.11	12491.51
	3		0.79	1.10	2650.00	2319.28	4704.83	15200.00	14074.07	4256.00	3724.85	15054.05
	4		0.74	1.16	2650.00	2254.86	6959.68	15200.00	14074.07	4104.00	3492.05	17541.71
	5		0.68	1.22	2650.00	2192.22	9151.90	15200.00	14074.07	3952.00	3269.30	19956.67
	6		0.63	1.28	2650.00	2131.33	11283.23	15200.00	14074.07	3800.00	3056.24	22301.06
	7		0.58	1.34	2650.00	2072.12	13355.35	15200.00	14074.07	3648.00	2852.49	24576.93
	8		0.54	1.41	2650.00	2014.56	15369.91	15200.00	14074.07	3496.00	2657.70	26786.28
	9		0.50	1.48	2650.00	1958.60	17328.52	15200.00	14074.07	3344.00	2471.54	28931.05
	10		0.46	1.55	2650.00	1904.20	19232.71	15200.00	14074.07	3192.00	2293.66	31013.13
	11		0.43	1.63	2650.00	1851.30	21084.02	15200.00	14074.07	3040.00	2123.76	33034.33
	12		0.40	1.71	2650.00	1799.88	22883.90	15200.00	14074.07	2888.00	1961.53	34996.44

(Continued)

TABLE 6.32 (CONTINUED)

Life Cycle Costing for Lighting – Option 2

Alternative Lighting Design Case for Villa Project

Time			Factors		Operation and Maintenance Cost (OC)			Initial Cost (IC)		Salvage Value at a Particular Year	PV of Salvage Value	Total LCC
Time Period	nth Year		Discounting Factor	Inflation Factor	Future OC in nth Year	PV of Any Year	Total PV Incurred	IC in nth Year	PV of Any Year			
			$1/(1+8/100)^n$	$(1+5/100)^{(n-1)}$	USD	USD	USD	USD	USD	USD	USD	USD
A			B	C	D	$E = D \times B \times C$	$F = E +$ last year's F	G	H	I	$J = I \times B \times C$	$K = H+F-J$
13			0.37	1.80	2650.00	1749.88	24633.78	15200.00	14074.07	2736.00	1806.67	36901.18
14			0.34	1.89	2650.00	1701.27	26335.05	15200.00	14074.07	2584.00	1658.90	38750.22
15			0.32	1.98	2650.00	1654.02	27989.07	15200.00	14074.07	2432.00	1517.95	40545.19
16			0.29	2.08	2650.00	1608.07	29597.14	15200.00	14074.07	2280.00	1383.55	42287.66
17			0.27	2.18	2650.00	1563.40	31160.54	15200.00	14074.07	2128.00	1255.44	43979.17
18			0.25	2.29	2650.00	1519.97	32680.52	15200.00	14074.07	1976.00	1133.38	45621.20
19			0.23	2.41	2650.00	1477.75	34158.27	15200.00	14074.07	1824.00	1017.14	47215.20
20			0.21	2.53	2650.00	1436.70	35594.97	15200.00	14074.07	1672.00	906.48	48762.57
21			0.20	2.65	2650.00	1396.80	36991.77	15200.00	14074.07	1520.00	801.18	50264.66
22			0.18	2.79	2650.00	1358.00	38349.76	15200.00	14074.07	1368.00	701.03	51722.81
23			0.17	2.93	2650.00	1320.27	39670.04	15200.00	14074.07	1216.00	605.83	53138.28
24			0.16	3.07	2650.00	1283.60	40953.64	15200.00	14074.07	1064.00	515.38	54512.34
25			0.15	3.23	2650.00	1247.94	42201.58	15200.00	14074.07	912.00	429.48	55846.18

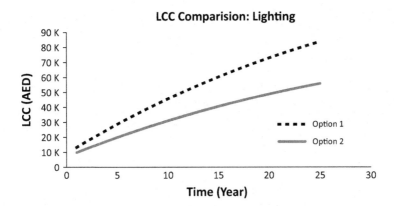

FIGURE 6.7
Comparison of Life Cycle Cost for Lighting System

Conclusion

It is found that option 2 (i.e., combination of lamps for lighting) is more cost-effective with respect to LCC analysis. Hence, the project design team has decided to go ahead with option 2.

7

Project Management Decisions

The general approach for making project management decisions consists of the steps such as identifying the problem, defining the goals to mitigate the problem, gathering information needed to make a rational decision, generating all the alternatives to solve the problem, analyzing alternatives, and making the sensible decision.

In project management, decisions need to be taken quite often. Exploring alternatives and analyzing them objectively is essential to make the best decision. LCCA plays a crucial role in these decision-making processes.

MAKE-OR-BUY

Making the decision to manufacture a product internally versus buying it from a third-party provider is known as a make-or-buy decision. Make-or-buy decisions, like outsourcing choices, involve weighing the benefits and costs of producing something internally versus purchasing it from a third party. All associated costs, including direct and indirect costs for procurement and the costs throughout the life cycle or a reasonable period, should be taken into account in a make-or-buy analysis.

Case Study

A chemical process plant in the United Kingdom needs a certain amount of resin for a particular operation. There is a proposal to install a resin preparation plant so that there is no requirement to buy it from the market. Before initiating the project to install a resin preparation plant, senior management wanted to carry out a make-or-buy decision to evaluate the

   DOI: 10.4324/9781003462330-8

feasibility of the new proposed plant with respect to buying the resin from the available market.

LCCA is carried out in addition to reviewing various other aspects to evaluate the make-or-buy decision.

Options for LCCA are as follows:

Option 1 – Buy Resin from Market:

Lack of internal expertise, low volume needs, and company's strategy for not entering into non-core activities are some of the factors that led the management to think buying resin rather than producing it.

Option 2 – Set up a Resin Preparation Plant:

Setting up a resin preparation plant will provide an opportunity for the company to in-house production of resin by using internal resources, without utilizing any facilities from outside the organization. As it will reduce the company's dependency on external agencies for the supply of resin, management doesn't want to reject the option of setting up a resin preparation plant straightway without proper analysis.

Input for LCCA:

Cost estimate values for option 1 (i.e., buy resin from the market) are provided in Table 7.1.

Cost estimate values for option 2 (i.e., set up a resin preparation plant) are provided in Table 7.2.

A summary of the cost element for both options is provided in Table 7.3 (for option 1) and Table 7.4 (for option 2).

TABLE 7.1

Cost Estimate Values for Option 1

	Buy Resin From Market		
A	Resin requirement for operation	0.804	TPH (Ton per hour)
B	Plant in operation	10	hours/day
C	Resin requirement per day (C = A × B)	8.041	TPD (Ton per Day)
D	Yearly operation	300	Days
E	Yearly resin requirement for the chemical plant (E = C × D)	2412.225	Ton
F	Price of resin	115	GBP/Ton
G	Resin storage cost (store room cost of GBP 3000 per month × 12 months)	36000	GBP/year
H	Total yearly cost of resin (H = E × F + G)	313406	GBP

TABLE 7.2

Cost Estimate Values for Option 2

Set up a Resin Preparation Plant			
Initial Cost			
Design and supply cost of the resin preparation plant	1,000,000	GBP	Based on the budgetary quote from the original equipment manufacturer
Erection cost of the resin preparation plant	400,000	GBP	
Total – Initial Cost	1,400,000	GBP	
Operation and Maintenance (O&M)			
1	Labour/workman/staff			
1a	No. of staff	1	No	
1b	Daily labour engagement in the new automated plant	2	Hours	
1c	Plant in operation	300	Days in a year	
1d	Hourly rate for labour	30	GBP	
	Total annual manpower cost	18,000	GBP	Total Annual Manpower cost = 1a × 1b × 1c × 1d
2	Electricity power requirement			
2a	Total electrical power requirement for new plant	32	KW	Estimated value based on the budgetary quote from the original equipment manufacturer
2b	Total no of days the plant is in operation	300	Days	
2c	Plant in operation	10	hours/day	
2d	Annual consumption	96,000	KWh	Annual consumption = 2a × 2b × 2c
2e	Electricity rate	0.1	GBP/KWh	
	Total annual electricity cost	9,600	GBP	Annual electricity cost = 2d × 2e
3	Total annual spare and maintenance cost	28,000	GBP	Estimated value based on the budgetary quote from the original equipment manufacturer
4	Raw material			
4a	Raw material rate	20	GBP/ton	
4b	Total raw material requirement	3,000	ton	
	Total annual raw material cost	60,000	GBP	
	Total – O&M	115,600		

TABLE 7.3

Cost Summary for Option 1

	Buy Resin From Market			
	Initial Cost			
Sl. No.	Cost Element	Value (in GBP)	Time Phase	Remarks
1	Design and development (D)	0		
2	Investment in asset (A)	0		
3	Installation (I)	0		
	Total	0		
	Operation and Maintenance Cost			
Sl. No.	Cost Element	Value (in GBP)/Year	Time Phase	Remarks
1	Labour (L)	0		
2	Energy/operational (E)	0		
3	Spare and maintenance (S)	0		
4	Resin procurement and storage (M)	313,406		
	Total	313,406		

TABLE 7.4

Cost Summary for Option 2

	Set up a Resin Preparation Plant			
	Initial Cost			
Sl. No.	Cost Element	Value (in GBP)	Time Phase	Remarks
1	Design and development (D)	0		OEM item
2	Investment in asset (A)	1,000,000		
3	Installation (I)	400,000		
	Total	1,400,000	1 year	
	Operation and Maintenance Cost			
Sl. No.	Cost Element	Value (in GBP)/Year	Time Phase	Remarks
1	Labour (L)	18,000		
2	Energy/operational (E)	9,600		
3	Spare and maintenance (S)	28,000		
4	Raw material (M)	60,000		
	Total	115,600	15 years	

Output for LCCA:

The Life Cycle Cost estimation for the option of buying resin is provided in Table 7.5.

The Life Cycle Cost estimation for the new proposed resin preparation plant is stipulated in Table 7.6.

A comparison of LCC for both options is presented in Figure 7.1.

From LCC of both the options, it is understood that setting up a new resin preparation plant will be viable after the ninth year. Considering the same, it is decided to go ahead with buying resin from the market instead of installing a new resin preparation plant.

BREAK EVEN POINT

For project decision-making, an assessment of the expected profitability of the project outcome is required, in addition to evaluating the most feasible alternative solution. If the output level and expected income generation for each choice vary, the Life Cycle Profit for each option needs to be calculated.

In case the expected output and revenue generation for all options are the same, the most feasible solution in terms of LCC may be chosen, and the Life Cycle Profit can be calculated for the chosen option only.

In the Case Study for LCCA in Chapter 4, option 1 (i.e., the sophisticated CNC machine) was the most feasible solution and selected for implementation. The year-wise generated revenue and profit can be assessed for option 1 by using the principle of present value.

Life Cycle Profit

Revenue generation from new machines is estimated as follows:

A. No of machine:	3
B. No of working days:	340 Days/year
C. Daily production per machine as per market demand:	18.63 Ton/day
D. Annual production per machine ($D = B \times C$):	6334.2 Ton/year
E. Rate of finished product as per market survey:	4000 USD/ton
F. Revenue from each machine ($F = D \times E/106$):	25.3 USD/year
G. Revenue from three machine ($G = F \times A$):	76 USD/year

TABLE 7.5

Life Cycle Costing for Option 1

						Buy Resin from Market						
Time	Factors		Operation and Maintenance Cost (OC)			Initial Cost (IC)		Salvage Value at Particular Year	PV of Salvage Value	Total LCC	Total LCC
Time Period	Discounting Factor	Inflation Factor	Future OC at nth Year	PV of Any Year	Total PV Incurred	IC at nth Year	PV of Any Year				
nth Year	$1/(1+8/100)^n$	$(1+5/100)^{(n-1)}$	GBP	GBP	GBP	GBP	GBP	GBP	GBP	GBP	Mil GBP
A	B	C	D	$E = D \times B \times C$	$F = E + \text{last Year's } F$	G	$H = G \times B \times C$	I	$J = I \times B \times C$	$K = H + F - J$	
1	0.93	1.00	313406	–	–	–	–	–	–	–	–
2	0.86	1.05	313406	282130	282130	–	–	–	–	282130	0.28
3	0.79	1.10	313406	274293	556423	–	–	–	–	556423	0.56
4	0.74	1.16	313406	266674	823096	–	–	–	–	823096	0.82
5	0.68	1.22	313406	259266	1082362	–	–	–	–	1082362	1.08
6	0.63	1.28	313406	252064	1334426	–	–	–	–	1334426	1.33
7	0.58	1.34	313406	245062	1579489	–	–	–	–	1579489	1.58
8	0.54	1.41	313406	238255	1817744	–	–	–	–	1817744	1.82
9	0.50	1.48	313406	231637	2049381	–	–	–	–	2049381	2.05
10	0.46	1.55	313406	225203	2274583	–	–	–	–	2274583	2.27
11	0.43	1.63	313406	218947	2493530	–	–	–	–	2493530	2.49
12	0.40	1.71	313406	212865	2706395	–	–	–	–	2706395	2.71
13	0.37	1.80	313406	206952	2913347	–	–	–	–	2913347	2.91
14	0.34	1.89	313406	201203	3114551	–	–	–	–	3114551	3.11
15	0.32	1.98	313406	195614	3310165	–	–	–	–	3310165	3.31

Note: Salvage Value can be put as "0" in case it has to be ignored

TABLE 7.6

Life Cycle Costing for Option 2

	Factors		Operation and Maintenance Cost (OC)			Initial Cost (IC)		Salvage Value in a Particular Year	PV of Salvage Value	Total LCC	Total LCC
Time			Set up a Resin Preparation Plant								
Time Period	Discounting Factor	Inflation Factor	Future OC in the nth Year	PV of Any Year	Total PV Incurred	IC in the nth Year	PV of Any Year			Total LCC	Total LCC
			GBP	GBP	GBP	GBP	GBP	GBP	GBP	GBP	mil GBP
nth Year	$1/(1+8/100)^n$	$(1+5/100)^{(n-1)}$		$E = D \times B \times C$	$F = E + $ last Year's F		$H = G \times B \times C$		$J = I \times B \times C$	$K = H + F - J$	
A	B	C	D	E	F	G	H	I	J	K	
1	0.93	1.00	–	–	–	1400000	1296296	–	–	1296296	1.30
2	0.86	1.05	115600	104064	104064	1400000	1296296	–	–	1400360	1.40
3	0.79	1.10	115600	101173	205237	1400000	1296296	–	–	1501533	1.50
4	0.74	1.16	115600	98363	303600	1400000	1296296	–	–	1599896	1.60
5	0.68	1.22	115600	95630	399230	1400000	1296296	–	–	1695526	1.70
6	0.63	1.28	115600	92974	492204	1400000	1296296	–	–	1788500	1.79
7	0.58	1.34	115600	90391	582596	1400000	1296296	–	–	1878892	1.88
8	0.54	1.41	115600	87881	670476	1400000	1296296	–	–	1966773	1.97
9	0.50	1.48	115600	85439	755916	1400000	1296296	–	–	2052212	2.05
10	0.46	1.55	115600	83066	838982	1400000	1296296	–	–	2135278	2.14
11	0.43	1.63	115600	80759	919741	1400000	1296296	–	–	2216037	2.22
12	0.40	1.71	115600	78515	998256	1400000	1296296	–	–	2294552	2.29
13	0.37	1.80	115600	76334	1074590	1400000	1296296	–	–	2370887	2.37
14	0.34	1.89	115600	74214	1148804	1400000	1296296	–	–	2445101	2.45
15	0.32	1.98	115600	72153	1220957	1400000	1296296	–	–	2517253	2.52

Note: Salvage Value can be put as "0" in case it has to be ignored

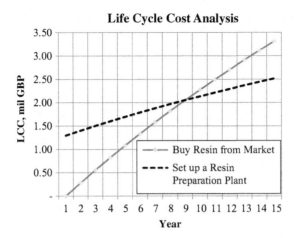

FIGURE 7.1

Life Cycle Cost Estimate Comparison

TABLE 7.7

Calculation for Life Cycle Revenue

	Revenue Generation by Using the Selected Option (i.e., Sophisticated CNC machine)					
	Factors		Revenue Generation			
Time Period	Discounting Factor	Inflation Factor	Future revenue Generation at nth Year	PV of Any Year	Total PV Incurred	Total Life Cycle Revenue
nth year	$1/(1 + 8/100)^n$	$(1 + 5/100)^{(n-1)}$	USD	USD	USD	USD
A	B	C	D	$E = D \times B \times C$	$F = E +$ last year's F	$H = F$
1	0.93	1	0	0	0	0.00
2	0.86	1.05	76.00	68.42	68.42	68.42
3	0.79	1.10	76.00	66.52	134.93	134.93
4	0.74	1.16	76.00	64.67	199.60	199.60
5	0.68	1.22	76.00	62.87	262.47	262.47
6	0.63	1.28	76.00	61.12	323.59	323.59
7	0.58	1.34	76.00	59.43	383.02	383.02
8	0.54	1.41	76.00	57.78	440.80	440.80
9	0.50	1.48	76.00	56.17	496.97	496.97
10	0.46	1.55	76.00	54.61	551.58	551.58

All cost values in million USD

As per the current strategy, the machines will be in production till tenth year.

The Life Cycle Revenue for option 1 is evaluated as per Table 7.7.

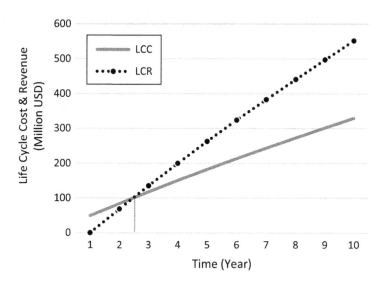

FIGURE 7.2
Comparison of Life Cycle Cost and Life Cycle Revenue

The year-wise Life Cycle Cost as per Table 4.3 and Life Cycle Revenue as per Table 7.7 are plotted in a graph. A comparison of Life Cycle Cost and Life Cycle Revenue is presented in Figure 7.2. The Break Even Point is found between the second and third year from the inception of the project.

The Life Cycle Profit is evaluated in Table 7.8 based on the calculated Life Cycle Cost and Life Cycle Revenue. It is observed that the profit is estimated from the third year onward which is in line with the representation of Figure 7.2.

Opportunity Cost

The potential gains that an individual, investor, or corporation forego while choosing one alternative over another are referred to as opportunity costs.

Instead of investing the initial money and Operation and Maintenance Cost year-on-year basis, the whole amount could have been kept in a bank account. The estimated bank interest is the Opportunity Cost for

TABLE 7.8

Calculation for Life Cycle Profit

Time Period	Year-wise Life Cycle Cost (As Per Table 4.3)	Year-wise Life Cycle Revenue (As Per Figure 7.2)	Year-wise Life Cycle Profit	Total Cumulative Life Cycle Profit
*n*th Year	USD	USD	USD	USD
A	B	C	D = C - B	E = D + Last Year's E
1	48.98	0.00	-48.98	-48.98
2	83.73	68.42	-15.31	-64.30
3	117.51	134.93	17.42	-46.88
4	150.36	199.60	49.24	2.37
5	182.29	262.47	80.18	82.55
6	213.33	323.59	110.26	192.81
7	243.52	383.02	139.51	332.31
8	272.86	440.80	167.94	500.25
9	301.39	496.97	195.58	695.83
10	329.13	551.58	222.45	918.28

the selected option. The detailed calculation for the Opportunity Cost is presented in Table 7.9.

A comparison of Life Cycle Profit and Opportunity Cost is presented in Figure 7.3. It is visible that investment in option 1 is an economically viable solution which has the potential to earn benefits.

For simplicity, only bank interest rates are considered in the example given in Table 7.9. However, instead of using bank interest rates to calculate opportunity costs, the weighted average cost of capital (WACC) may also be used. A firm's cost of capital is represented by its WACC which represents a proportional weight to each category of capital. WACC is commonly used as a benchmark rate by businesses and investors to determine the viability of a project.

WEIGHTED AVERAGE COST OF CAPITAL

The average of all capital expenses that a company incurs is shown by the term weighted average cost of capital (WACC). Long-term liabilities and debts, such as preferred and common stocks and bonds

TABLE 7.9

Calculation for Opportunity Cost

Time Period	Initial Cost	O&M Cost	Year-wise Interest Rate on Initial Cost	Year-wise Interest Rate on O&M Cost (Note: Interest Rate 8%)								
			Year	Year								
nth Year			1	2	3	4	5	6	7	8	9	10
	USD	USD	USD	USD								
A	B	C	$D = (B + \text{Previous Year D}) \times \text{Interest Rate}$	$E = (C + \text{Previous Year E}) \times \text{Interest Rate}$								
1	52.90		4.2									
2		38.60	4.6	3.1								
3		38.60	4.9	3.3	3.1							
4		38.60	5.3	3.6	3.3	3.1						
5		38.60	5.8	3.9	3.6	3.3	3.1					
6		38.60	6.2	4.2	3.9	3.6	3.3	3.1				
7		38.60	6.7	4.5	4.2	3.9	3.6	3.3	3.1			
8		38.60	7.3	4.9	4.5	4.2	3.9	3.6	3.3	3.1		
9		38.60	7.8	5.3	4.9	4.5	4.2	3.9	3.6	3.3	3.1	
10		38.60	8.5	5.7	5.3	4.9	4.5	4.2	3.9	3.6	3.3	3.1

Cumulative Initial Cost Adding Interest Rate	Cumulative O&M Cost Adding Interest Rate									Year-Wise total Interest Earned
Year	Year									
1	2	3	4	5	6	7	8	9	10	
USD	USD									USD
$F = (D + \text{Previous Year F})$	$G = (E \text{ of Respective Year} + \text{Previous Year G})$									$H = D + \text{Sum of } E$
57.1										4.2
61.7	41.7									7.7
66.6	45.0	41.7								11.4
72.0	48.6	45.0	41.7							15.4
77.7	52.5	48.6	45.0	41.7						19.7
83.9	56.7	52.5	48.6	45.0	41.7					24.3
90.7	61.3	56.7	52.5	48.6	45.0	41.7				29.4
97.9	66.2	61.3	56.7	52.5	48.6	45.0	41.7			34.8
105.7	71.4	66.2	61.3	56.7	52.5	48.6	45.0	41.7		40.7
114.2	77.2	71.4	66.2	61.3	56.7	52.5	48.6	45.0	3.1	47.0

TABLE 7.9 (CONTINUED)

Calculation for Opportunity Cost

Discounting Factor	Inflation Factor	NPV of Year-Wise Total Interest Earned	NPV of Cumulative Interest Earned
$1/(1+8/100)^n$	$(1+5/100)^{(n-1)}$	USD	USD
I	J	K = J X I X J	L = K + Previous Year L
0.9	1.0	3.9	3.9
0.9	1.1	6.9	10.8
0.8	1.1	9.9	20.8
0.7	1.2	13.1	33.8
0.7	1.2	16.3	50.1
0.6	1.3	19.6	69.7
0.6	1.3	23.0	92.6
0.5	1.4	26.5	119.1
0.5	1.5	30.1	149.2
0.5	1.6	33.8	182.9

All cost values in million USD

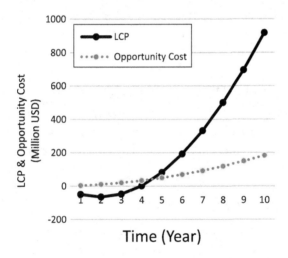

FIGURE 7.3
Comparison of Life Cycle Profit and Opportunity Cost

that businesses issue to shareholders and capital investors, can be included in capital costs. The WACC uses the weighted average of each source of capital for which a company is responsible.

The formula for calculating WACC is given in Equation 7.1.

$$\text{WACC} = \left(\frac{E}{V} \times R_e\right) + \left(\frac{D}{V} \times R_d \times \left(1 - T_c\right)\right) \qquad (7.1)$$

Where,

E = Market value of the company's equity.
D = Market value of the company's debt.
V = E + D.
R_e = Cost of equity.
R_d = Cost of debt.
T_c = Corporate tax rate.

MARKET VALUE OF COMPANY'S EQUITY

Equity is the amount of money invested in or owned by a company's owner. The total value of a company's equity, often known as its market capitalization, is its market value of equity. The number of outstanding shares multiplied by the current share price yields the market value of the equity.

MARKET VALUE OF THE COMPANY'S DEBT

The amount of bank debt that businesses have is referred to as their market value of debt. The market value of debt, which is different from the balance sheet book value, refers to the price at which investors would be willing to purchase a company's debt.

COST OF EQUITY

The cost of equity is the rate of return paid to equity investors by a corporation. The cost of equity is used by a company to evaluate the relative attractiveness of investments, including both internal projects and external acquisition options.

The cost of equity can be calculated by various methods. One of the methods for calculating the cost of equity is the Dividend Capitalization Model as shown in Equation 7.2.

$$R_e = \left(D_1 / P_0\right) + g \qquad (7.2)$$

Where,

R_e = Cost of Equity.

D_1 = Dividends/shares next year.

P_0 = Current share price.

g = Dividend growth rate.

COST OF DEBT

The effective interest rate that a company pays on its debts, such as bonds and loans, is referred to as the cost of debt. Not only does the cost of debt reflect a company's default risk, but it also reflects market interest rates.

CORPORATE TAX RATE

Corporate tax is a direct tax placed on a company's net income or profit from its operations. The corporate tax rate is the rate at which the corporate tax is levied.

ASSESSMENT OF PROJECT DELAY

A project delay is typically an issue that causes businesses to go over budget, miss deadlines, and sometimes derail projects. It can have a significant impact on costs and timelines. As a result of the delay, the owner loses money, time, and other resources. Delays affect contractors as well.

How to assess the impact of a project delay?

Time Impact Analysis (TIA) or Update Impact Analysis (UIA) is well-known and widely used schedule delay analysis methodology. It is widely accepted as the preferred method to demonstrate a contractor's entitlement to a time extension or the owner's justification for receiving liquidated damages.

In case of project delay, organizations normally calculate additional expenditure and opportunity loss incurred due to delay. Accordingly, the organization calculates the total cost and opportunity loss incurred in the project life cycle. Organizations also calculate revenue, i.e., earnings, if any, within the project life cycle (more applicable for the contractors who receive part payments during the project life cycle). Then the total expenditure and earnings are compared to understand the financial impact of the delay.

However, money is time-dependent. For a long delay, a simple summation or deduction of monetary values cannot give a true picture. Economic impact due to project delay can be calculated by using the Life Cycle Cost Analysis methodology. The present value of the cost or earnings throughout the project life cycle can be calculated to understand the impact of the delay.

Case Study

An India-based contracting company involved in engineering, procurement, and construction management (EPCM) has been assigned by owner's company to execute a small power plant project in India. The original schedule of the project was 3 years. The contracting company initially spent a year time for receiving the go-ahead from the owner by involving the marketing team, buying new software to enhance capabilities, etc. The financial data related to the above project for the EPCM company is given in the Table 7.10.

TABLE 7.10

Financial Data for EPCM Company

Project	Power Plant Project	
	Cost in INR	Time scale
Total order value to the EPCM company [A]	208,960,600	
Estimated initial pre-project costs such as cost for tendering, new software purchase, new recruitment, etc. [B]	2,022,340	12 months (1 year)
Estimated total cost for EPCM during the project lifetime, such as employee salary for engineering and project management, cost for a site office, and travelling, etc. [C]	191,666,213	24 months (2 years), i.e., project lifetime
Estimated profit [A - (B + C)]	15,272,047	

The project was supposed to be completed in 3 years, which includes the initial 1 year for marketing, etc. However, the project execution was slow from the beginning and at the end of the second year; the owner was not able to drive the project further due to different reasons. At the end of the second year, the EPCM company's management wanted to evaluate the economic impact of its business for the delay in different scenarios, considering the project would be completed in 4 years or 5 years. Actual expenditures in the first year and second years were INR 2,022,340 and INR 35,589,951, respectively.

As the project got delayed, an analysis was carried out for three different scenarios as per Table 7.11. These scenarios are based on expected project completion in 3 years, 4 years, and 5 years from inception.

EPCM company estimated the revised cost to complete the project in different scenarios.

The cost element for different options is provided in Tables 7.12, 7.13, and 7.14.

TABLE 7.11

Different Scenarios Considered for Expected Project Completion

Description	Project Lifetime		Remarks
Option 1	Project Lifetime (years):	3	Base case (as per project schedule)
Option 2	Project lifetime (years):	4	
Option 3	Project lifetime (years):	5	

TABLE 7.12

Estimated Cost Element for Option 1 (Considering Project Completion in 3 Years)

		Option 1					
		Year-wise Cost Distribution					
Sl. No.	Cost Element	1 (Pre-project Time)	2	3	4	5	Total Cost (in INR)
		Cost (in INR)/Year					
A	Total Initial Cost	2,022,340 (actual cost incurred)	–	–	–	–	2,022,340
B	Total Operating Cost		35,589,951 (actual cost incurred)	156,076,262 (estimated cost)	–	–	191,666,213

TABLE 7.13

Estimated Cost Element for Option 2 (Considering Project Completion in 4 Years)

		Option 2					
		Year-wise Cost Distribution					
		1 (Pre-project time)	**2**	**3**	**4**	**5**	**Total Cost (in INR)**
Sl. No.	**Cost Element**	Cost (in INR)/Year					
A	Total Initial Cost	2,022,340 (actual cost incurred)	–	–	–	–	2,022,340
B	Total Operating Cost		35,589,951 (actual cost incurred)	23,873,900 (updated estimated cost)	151,354,523 (updated estimated cost)	–	210,818,374

TABLE 7.14

Estimated Cost Element for Option 3 (Considering Project Completion in 5 Years)

		Option 3					
		Year-wise Cost Distribution					
		1 (Pre-project Time)	**2**	**3**	**4**	**5**	**Total Cost (in INR)**
Sl. No.	**Cost Element**	Cost (in INR)/Year					
A	Total Initial Cost	2,022,340 (Actual cost incurred)					2,022,340
B	Total Operating Cost		35,589,951 (actual cost incurred)	23,873,900 (updated estimated cost)	125,358,654 (updated estimated cost)	49,179,692 (updated estimated cost)	234,002,197

By applying the principle of Life Cycle Cost Analysis, the project cost was evaluated in the life cycle period for all three options considering the discount rate as 8% and inflation rate as 5%. Tables 7.15, 7.16, and 7.17 depict the outcome of the evaluation for options 1, 2, and 3, respectively. A comparison of the life cycle project cost for all three options is presented in Figure 7.4.

TABLE 7.15

Life Cycle Cost Calculation for Option 1 (Considering Project Completion in 3 Years)

											3 (Base Case)
				Option 1							
				Project Lifetime (years):							
Time	Factors			Operation Cost (OC)			Initial Cost (IC)		Salvage Value at Particular Year (Not Applicable)	PV of Salvage Value (Not Applicable)	Total LCC
Time Period	Discounting Factor	Inflation Factor	Future OC in the nth Year	PV of Any Year	Total PV Incurred	IC in the nth Year	PV of Any Year				
			INR	INR	INR	INR	INR	INR	INR	INR	INR
nth Year	$1/(1+8/100)^{n}$	$(1+5/100)^{(n-1)}$	INR	INR	INR	INR	INR	INR	INR	INR	INR
A	B	C	D	$E = D \times B \times C$	$F = E + $ last Year's F	G	H	I	$J = I \times B \times C$		$K = H + F - J$
1	0.93	1	0	0	0	2022340	1872537	0	0		1872537
2	0.86	1.05	35589951	32038279	32038279	2022340	1872537	0	0		33910816
3	0.79	1.10	156076262	136597952	168863231	2022340	1872537	0	0		170508768

TABLE 7.16

Life Cycle Cost Calculation for Option 2 (Considering Project Completion in 4 Years)

| | | | | | | | | | | Option 2 | |
| | | | | | | | | | | Project Lifetime (Years): | 4 |
Time	Factors		Operation Cost (OC)			Initial Cost (IC)		Salvage Value at Particular Year (Not Applicable)	PV of Salvage Value	Total LCC
Time Period	Discounting Factor	Inflation Factor	Future OC at nth Year	PV of Any Year	Total PV Incurred	IC at nth Year	PV of Any Year	Year	Year	
nth Year	$1/(1+8/100)^n$	$(1+5/100)^{(n-1)}$	INR	INR	INR		INR	INR	INR	INR
A	B	C	D	$E = D \times C$	$F = E + \text{Last Year's F}$	G	H	I	$J = I \times B \times C$	$K = H + F - J$
1	0.93	1	0	0	0	2022340	1872537	0	0	1872537
2	0.86	1.05	35589951	32038279	32038279	2022340	1872537	0	0	33910816
3	0.79	1.10	23873900	20894438	52932717	2022340	1872537	0	0	54805254
4	0.74	1.16	151354523	128785889	181718606	2022340	1872537	0	0	183591143

TABLE 7.17

Life Cycle Cost Calculation for Option 3 (Considering Project Completion in 5 Years)

Time	Factors		Operation Cost (OC)			Initial Cost (IC)		Salvage Value at Particular Year (Not Applicable)	PV of Salvage Value	Total LCC
										Option 3
										5
					Project Lifetime (Years):					
Time Period	Discounting Factor	Inflation Factor	Future OC at nth Year	PV of Any Year	Total PV Incurred	IC at nth Year	PV of Any Year	Salvage Value at Particular Year	PV of Salvage Value	Total LCC
					INR		INR	INR	INR	INR
nth Year	$1/(1+8/100)^n$	$(1+5/100)^{(n-1)}$	INR	INR	INR					
A	B	C	D	$E = D \times B \times C$	$F = E + $ Last Year's F	G	H	I	$J = I \times B \times C$	$K = H + F + J$
1	0.93	1	0	0	0	2022340	1872537	0	0	1872537
2	0.86	1.05	35589951	32038279	32038279	2022340	1872537	0	0	33910816
3	0.79	1.10	23873900	20894438	52932717	2022340	1872537	0	0	54805254
4	0.74	1.16	125358654	106666291	159599008	2022340	1872537	0	0	161471545
5	0.68	1.22	49179692	40684054	200283063	2022340	1872537	0	0	202155600

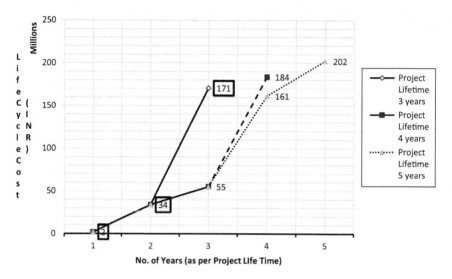

FIGURE 7.4

Life Cycle Cost for Different Scenarios (Option 1, 2, and 3)

TABLE 7.18

Revenue Forecast for Different Scenarios

Sl. No. Option	Cost Element		Total Order Value	Year-wise Revenue Distribution					Total Revenue
				1	**2**	**3**	**4**	**5**	
1	Project Lifetime (years):	2	208960600	–	94032270	114928330			208960600
2	Project Lifetime (years):	3	208960600	–	94032270	52240150	62688180		208960600
3	Project Lifetime (years):	4	208960600	–	94032270	52240150	31344090	31344090	208960600

The company further decided to cross-check the year-wise revenue generation pattern for different options for comparing the project Life Cycle Cost with the revenue forecast.

The year-wise estimated revenue for three options is provided in Table 7.18.

Estimated revenue was evaluated in the life cycle period for all three options considering the discount rate as 8% and inflation rate as 5%. The principle of Life Cycle Cost Analysis was adopted. Tables 7.19, 7.20, and 7.21

TABLE 7.19

Life Cycle Revenue Earning for Option 1 (Considering Project Completion in 3 Years)

			Option 1						
			Project Lifetime (Years):						3
Time	Factors			Revenue Earning (Value)			LD Clause (Cost)		
Time Period	Discounting Factor	Inflation Factor	Future OC in nth Year	PV of Any Year	Total PV Incurred	Salvage Value at a Particular Year	PV of Salvage Value	Total LCC
nth Year	$1/(1 + 8/100)^n$	$(1 + 5/100)^{(n-1)}$	INR	INR	INR	INR	INR	INR
A	B	C	D	$E = D \times B \times C$	$F = E + \text{Last Year's } F$	G	$H = I \times B \times C$	$I = F - H$
1	0.93	1	0	0	0	0	0	0
2	0.86	1.05	94032270	84648391	84648391	0	0	84648391
3	0.79	1.10	114928330	100585280	185233671	0	0	185233671

TABLE 7.20

Life Cycle Revenue Earning for Option 2 (Considering Project Completion in 4 Years)

					Option2				4
Time					Project Lifetime, (Years)				
	Factors			Revenue Earning (Value)			LD Clause (Cost)		
Time Period	Discounting Factor	Inflation Factor	Future OC at nth Year	PV of Any Year	Total PV Incurred	Salvage Value at Particular Year	PV of Salvage Value	Total LCC	
nth Year	$1/(1+8/100)^n$	$(1+5/100)^{(n-1)}$	INR	INR	INR	INR	INR	INR	
A	B	C	D	$E = D \times B \times C$	$F = E + $ last Year's F	G	$H = I \times B \times C$	$I = F-H$	
1	0.93	1	0	0	0	0	0	0	
2	0.86	1.05	94032270	84648391	84648391	0	0	84648391	
3	0.79	1.10	52240150	45720582	130368973	0	0	130368973	
4	0.74	1.16	62688180	53340678.6	183709651	0	0	183709651	

TABLE 7.21

Life Cycle Revenue Earning for Option 3 (Considering Project Completion in 5 Years)

				Option 3				
Time				Project Lifetime (Years)				5
	Factors		Revenue Earning (Value)			LD Clause (Cost)		
Time Period	Discounting Factor	Inflation Factor	Future OC at nth Year	PV of Any Year	Total PV Incurred	Salvage Value at Particular Year	PV of Salvage Value	Total LCC
nth Year	$1/(1 + 8/100)^n$	$(1 + 5/100)^{(n-1)}$	INR	INR	INR	INR	INR	INR
A	B	C	D	$E = D \times B \times C$	$F = E + $ Last Year's F	G	$H = I \times B \times C$	$I = F-H$
1	0.93	1	0	0	0	0	0	0
2	0.86	1.05	94032270	84648391	84648391	0	0	84648391
3	0.79	1.10	52240150	45720582	130368973	0	0	130368973
4	0.74	1.16	31344090	26670339.3	157039312	0	0	157039312
5	0.68	1.22	31344090	25929496.5	182968809	0	0	182968809

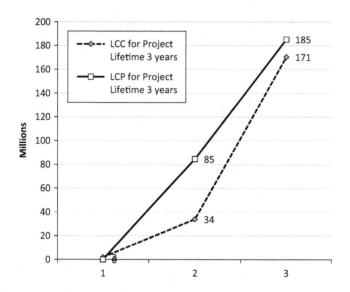

FIGURE 7.5

Comparison of Life Cycle Project Cost and Life Cycle Revenue for Option 1

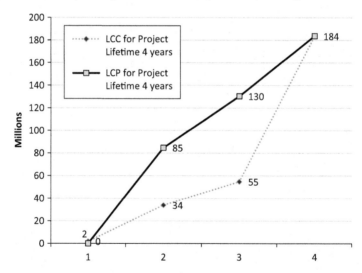

FIGURE 7.6

Comparison of Life Cycle Project Cost and Life Cycle Revenue for Option 2

depict the outcome of the evaluation for options 1, 2, and 3, respectively. A comparison of the project Life Cycle Cost and Life Cycle Revenue for all three options is presented in Figures 7.5, 7.6, and 7.7, respectively. As per Figure 7.5, if the project is completed within the scheduled timeframe

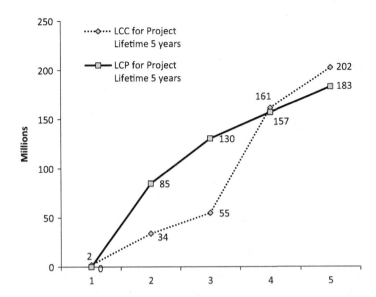

FIGURE 7.7
Comparison of Life Cycle Project Cost and Life Cycle Revenue for Option 3

of 3 years, then the contracting company can yield profit. If the project is completed in 4 years, then there will be an almost no-loss-no-gain situation for the contracting company as per Figure 7.6. However, if the project time further slipped for a year, then the EPCM company will incur an economic loss as per Figure 7.7.

8

Impact of Life Cycle Cost Analysis

What are the challenges of using Life Cycle Cost Analysis (LCCA)?

LCCA considers various logical approximations and assumptions. Due to this, the estimated results may not be very accurate in reality. However, it is also true that, as the same assumptions are implied to all the options, hence, the comparative results will provide a fairly accurate picture of the most viable option.

The life-cycle costing approach equitably distributes an asset's expense over multiple years. This never happens in reality.

According to the life cycle costing theory, an asset will continue to be just as productive after its initial purchase. Perhaps in reality it happens differently.

Also, many a time estimating operational costs is difficult due to the lack of data. The LCCA have to apply assumptions judiciously and logically.

Though there are a few challenges, LCCA is gaining importance as a decision-making tool because of the following reasons:

- The entire cost of ownership is examined and assessed by the LCCA. It translates all the tangible or intangible aspects of an asset into cost elements.
- It is easy to compare different options over a life cycle period as LCCA is holistic and easy to represent.
- With the growing importance of sustainable solutions, it is important to consider parameters like carbon footprint in business decision-making. LCCA can take it into account.
- Through LCCA, a realistic assessment of costs and revenue is possible within a specified life cycle span which can help to calculate the break-even point for business decision-making.

     DOI: 10.4324/9781003462330-9

LCCA is one of the useful tools for business decision-making, especially where different options are available to make appropriate assessments. In the modern business context, LCCA is helpful for sustainable business models.

SUSTAINABILITY TOOL

Sustainability is the ability to continuously support or maintain a process across time. Sustainability aims to prevent the depletion of physical or natural resources so that they remain usable in the future. The three pillars of sustainability are economy, environment, and society. Most of the time, there is structural tension between these three pillars as they are contradictory, and they have a tremendous impact on each other. Equilibrium is very much needed for sustainability. To measure and monitor the degree of equilibrium, Life Cycle Cost is a useful tool. It converts all the dimensions of any entity into cost figures over the life cycle and compares them with the available alternatives. It provides a fair amount of opportunity to evaluate all the possible options to choose the most feasible one. Life Cycle Costing (LCC) is one of the sustainability tools that concentrate on the construction and consumption of goods and services. LCC is an economic approach that sums up the total costs of a product, service, process, or activity discounted over its life cycle. It takes into account all possible parameters which impact the usage of the product. Capturing equivalent emission cost (say equivalent carbon footprint cost) incurred by an entity over its life cycle and evaluating the same along with other cost parameters makes the LCCA a useful sustainability tool. Equivalent carbon footprint is the quantity of carbon that equals the global warming potential of a specific mixture and amount of different greenhouse gases when measured over a specified timescale. This reflects the different global warming potentials of different greenhouse gases. LCC enables decision-makers to calculate this global warming potential in terms of cost and find out its impact along with other cost parameters such as operation and maintenance cost over the life cycle of the entity.

In a true sense, though LCCA is related to sustainability, they are not synonymous. LCCA is a cost-based quality assurance approach. The aim of LCCA is to identify the most cost-efficient solution. LCCA focuses on values that can be measured in cost figures. But LCCA does not consider subjective parameters such as comfort. The most cost-effective solution is not always the most environmentally best choice, as a sum of all other cost parameters can have a predominant effect than environmental cost. For instance, a building may use very little energy, yet its maintenance expenses may exceed the money it saves on energy. However, LCCA frequently identifies environmentally preferable options. In a nutshell, LCCA is an important tool that helps in pointing out the impact of different parameters associated with an entity and strikes a balance between economic concern and environmental issues.

> **A Simplified Example of Calculating Carbon Dioxide Emission Cost**
>
> In a heating system, there is an option to use natural gas as a fuel. The amount of carbon dioxide emission and subsequent cost element for using natural gas can be calculated as follows:
>
> a. Carbon dioxide emitted by using natural gas: 2.75 kg/kg of natural gas (as per scientific data)
> b. Amount of natural gas required as fuel: 11000 kg/hour (as per project-specific estimate)
> c. Amount of carbon dioxide emitted ($c = a \times b$): 30250 kg/hour
> d. Annual use of heating system: 330 days
> e. Daily usage of heating system: 24 hours @ 330 days
> f. Annual emission of carbon dioxide ($f = c \times d \times e/1000$): 239580 Ton/year
> g. Rate of carbon dioxide emission: 75 USD/Ton
> h. Cost of total carbon dioxide emission ($h = f \times g$): 17,968,500 USD/year.
>
> This annual cost for carbon dioxide emission can be used as one of the operating expense (OPEX) element for LCCA.

ASSET MANAGEMENT TOOL

Asset management is the principle of managing the physical assets of an organization to attain the stated outputs. Asset management emphasizes assessing the existing assets regularly. Based on the assessment, decisions for short-, medium-, and long-term investment plans for the various assets must be made, including deciding whether the existing asset can be utilized with some OPEX investment or replaced with capital expenditure (CAPEX). Needs and demand analysis is important to analyze the investment plan. As part of the needs analysis, deficiency or need is determined to achieve the intended purpose of the respective assets. Demand analysis critically reviews the finding of the needs analysis for various aspects and alternative scenarios. LCCA is one of the important tools in demand analysis where economic aspects of various alternatives are critically evaluated within the specified time frame for the asset or asset portfolio.

TOTAL PRODUCTIVE MAINTENANCE (TPM) TOOL

One of the pillars of TPM is Maintenance Prevention.

Early Management, Initial Phase Management, and Initial Flow Control are other terms for Maintenance Prevention.

Maintenance Prevention enhancements are largely based on learning from existing equipment and processes within the TPM pillar activities of Focused Improvement, Autonomous Maintenance, and Planned Maintenance.

Maintenance Prevention makes use of previous maintenance improvement activities' experience to ensure that new machinery reaches peak performance much sooner than usual.

Maintenance Prevention develops systems to reduce the time required for new product or equipment development, start-up, commissioning, and stabilization in order to maximize output quality and operating efficiency.

According to Maintenance Prevention, the new equipment must have the following features:

- Simple to use
- Simple to clean
- Simple to maintain
- Reliable
- Have quick set-up times

The goal of Maintenance Prevention is to reduce the equipment's Life Cycle Cost. Evaluation of alternatives considering LCCA is one of the important aspects of Maintenance Prevention.

PROJECT MANAGEMENT TOOL

A project can be divided into as many phases as desired. A project phase is a collection of project activities that finish in the completion of one or more planned deliverables which is linked to the ultimate objective of the project. At the end of a phase, the deliverables are reviewed by concerned stakeholders. This is commonly known as stage gate. Stakeholders used to review the pros and cons of the deliverables and decide if the project is to be further continued. During this review, different alternatives for various aspects are critically evaluated. In this context, Life Cycle Cost plays an important role in evaluating different alternatives. Also, during project execution, LCCA can be used for various purposes, such as to decide to make or buy a plan or to estimate the economic effect of a project delay.

LIFE CYCLE ASSESSMENT

The term Life Cycle Assessment (LCA) refers to the approach for evaluating the environmental effects related to each stage of the life cycle of an asset. A Life Cycle Assessment includes a complete inventory of the energy and materials needed throughout the value chain of the asset and estimates the related emissions to the environment (refer to Figure 8.1).

The objectives of LCA are as follows:

- To quantify all inputs and outputs of material flows in order to compare the whole spectrum of environmental consequences attributable to the asset.
- To evaluate the environmental impact of the product's material flows.
- To enhance procedures, back up policy, and offer a solid foundation for informed decisions.

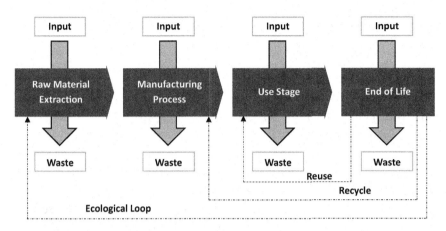

FIGURE 8.1
Life Cycle Assessment stage diagram

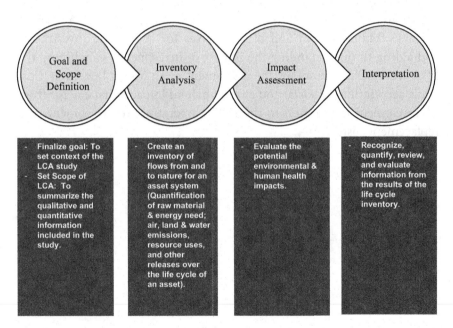

FIGURE 8.2
General phases of Life Cycle Assessment

LCA is carried out in four main interlinked iterative phases (refer to Figure 8.2):

a) Goal and scope definition
b) Inventory analysis
c) Impact assessment
d) Interpretation

The LCA was mainly used as a comparison tool, to compare an asset with available alternatives by assessing environmental impacts. However, its potential applications have been extended to encompass product development, marketing, strategic planning, consumer training, eco-labelling, and government policy.

LCA and LCCA are different in that LCA makes an effort to measure an asset's environmental impact at every stage of its life. In contrast, LCCA calculates the investment's whole financial impact over its lifetime. Although they approach it from different angles, LCA and LCCA are both valuable frameworks in and of themselves for comparing investments and aiding in understanding the impact of investments. Combining the LCA with LCCA allows for the assessment of an asset's Life Cycle Cost while accounting for social and environmental impacts that emerge from an investment in addition to the initial, operating, refurbishment, and replacement costs.

9

Life Cycle Cost Analysis Experiences

LCCA has been extensively followed in the United States since the 1960s. To improve its cost-effectiveness while making competitive awards, the US Department of Defense emphasized the creation and use of LCC. Gradually, from defense systems, LCC has expanded into industrial and consumer goods areas.

There are various models for LCCA. The majority of LCCA models were created using the resources and goals of the model creator. As a result, case-by-case models have been developed. The underlying goals of all the models are, nevertheless, quite similar to one another.

As all facets of our economy are currently getting more cost-conscious, life cycle expenses are gaining importance across all decision-making processes. Today more than ever, LCCA principles are being applied to every aspect of life, including the public and corporate sectors as well as non-profit organizations.

How are professionals, researchers, and students using LCCA?

Let us meet some interesting personalities across the globe to know their views and experiences on LCCA.

DR. DAVID HALLORAN

Chairman, Halloran Associates, Florida, USA

Dr. David G. Halloran earned his bachelor's degree in economics from Dartmouth College in 1953, with a winning senior thesis on the opinions of economist Dr. Maynard Keynes. From 1953 until 1961, Dr. Halloran served as a fighter pilot in the United States Navy. After that, he was in

DOI: 10.4324/9781003462330-10

the aerospace industry in Business Development jobs with business giants like Douglas, which became McDonnell Douglas, the Martin Marietta in international sales of defence products to NATO and US Allies.

Dr. Halloran is an ardent follower of the open market economy. He believes that an open market economy increases opportunity and prosperity globally, thereby fostering more security, innovation, and stability for everyone.

After retiring from Martin Marietta in 1988, he financed his own management consultancy company Halloran Associates in Florida. He also went back to college for his PhD at the University of Central Florida (UCF) to polish his mathematics and computer science. He implemented the concepts of simulation strategy in Halloran Associates and worked on Laplace Transformation to improve the transition accuracy of simulations. He has utilized Life Cycle Cost Analysis (LCCA) extensively for strategizing operations in the Aeroplane industry.

What is the importance of Life Cycle Cost Analysis in complex decision-making process?

Dr. Halloran: One of the greatest dangers in the assumption of a repetitive cost history during an identical production cycle of a product of identical design is the potential for change in the indirect variables impacting the production line such as power probes, personnel change or disease, governmental policies such as taxation impact, facility breakdown, and the greatest is the change in competitors pricing designed to acquire a greater share of the market. The thought process is similar to the application of succeeding differential equations at different phases of the simulation calculations that often can be resolved by the application of Laplace transforms. The bottom line is that each phase is a distinct entity and to determine actual costs, the LCCA data must be reviewed in micro detail and modified as necessary. Not doing so is one of the principal reasons businesses, particularly new ones, get clobbered in the market and take losses. Our experience with LCCA, a vital component of designing market and pricing strategy, has been to examine the architecture of the successful LCCA when compared to actuals, and then examine the performance and architectures of the successful LCCA to the new product or development activity. There will always be uncertainties in this phase which will require the planning for alternatives in the event the projections become erroneous.

LCCA is essentially a management tool that is becoming more and more applicable in the highly competitive world and is being used more and more in technology firms.

Being a management consultant, how has LCCA helped you in your work? Please provide some interesting real-life stories where crucial decisions were taken based on LCCA.

Dr. Halloran: While working with major American aerospace manufacturing corporations, we always used to say in our executive planning sessions that LCCA is vital not only to the performance of the existing contract or program but it is also important to evaluating our competitive position in the overall very aggressive marketplace in the free enterprise capitalistic economies as well as those economies that have dictatorial pricing policies established by non-free enterprises market systems.

Within free enterprise companies, there will always be a debate between the engineering, purchasing, manufacturing, cost accounting, and human resource elements that contribute to the LCC of a product. It is more applicable to the products of interest to the governments such as defense, communications, energy, and health and medical considerations that are highly technology-driven and have great impact due to economic fluctuations and unforeseen influences such as political decisions. While it is impossible to project with acceptable accuracy what the competition will do in X years, and each year is dynamic given the overall conditions of the economy and market, the LCCA of one's own organization must be constantly compared with the projected LCCA of the competition. The data on that competition can be derived from market intelligence to a degree, but more importantly, by the simulation of the competitor's projected LCC based on past experience.

The powerful influence of accurate simulation data and architecture that provides reasonable accuracy as to the projected competitive pricing advantage, or disadvantage, depending on the circumstances, comes into play here and is a very valuable but vulnerable area on which to base significant decisions based on comparative projected LCCA with competitive firms. It is this aspect of the utilization of projected LCCA of self versus projected LCCA of the competitors that the ICON model we developed became very useful to our clients.

That is a tough job that requires tapping many elements of the corporate structure and as the old saying goes "The Devil lies in the details" or as my German counterparts used to say "Der Teufel liegt im Detail."

I had an experience long ago with nailing the winning price on a major defense program that we had the absolute right answer. It was a program in the 50 million range and with the certainty of the accuracy of the winning competitive price after pursuing the foregone analysis, in the Board meeting the Vice President from our finance department suggested we add a couple of million more with this certainty of win. That astonished me and the CEO, a lifelong friend, and three of the Board members present; I strongly said that if we raise the price one penny more, we could not guarantee a win. A hush came over the room! We ultimately decided not to increase the price. We won the program! When our company had to recompete the program about seven years later, and I had retired by then and set up Halloran Associates, the company upped the price and lost! Trust the LCCA analysis for not only one's projected costs but also for competitive analysis.

I am sharing another experience where we have utilized LCCA extensively on behalf of Halloran Associates. Our experience is in the aerospace realm, but we have addressed many elements of that market and have found, for example, that alternative manufacturing processes, as a function of the position of the project in its time history, can yield illuminating insights. We had worked on a program for 19 years with one of our clients. It sold a product at the same average unit production price for 19 years (with higher margins!) with or without the effects of inflation, union demands for salary increases, the temptation to adopt new technology by reconfiguring the existing technology, and disruptions in the supply base. We have walked the line with our client to get an idea of what could be changed using the existing equipment, plant layout, people, etc. It is amazing what little adjustments can do to not only restrain cost growth but also to reduce it without further major investment. Probably the largest impact is a micro examination of the procurement process including "make or buy." Others have tried to compete with this client but have not been successful. LCCA was their ticket to extended life.

What are your views on the LCCA methodologies described in this book?
Dr. Halloran: The framework illustrated in this book is a very meticulous architectural strategy for LCCA which has been most helpful to me and my students and clients. I think the great lesson this LCCA framework teaches is the need to include complete detail in the analysis even though some aspects like discount rate and inflation rate may be intuitively

obvious. The impact of those rates is, of course, a function of the principal cost item with the relevant variances. The framework manifests complete discipline.

The framework for LCCA illustrated in this book has been most useful to our company, Halloran Associates, in two aspects:

First: Auditing the completeness of our existing LCCA strategies which we call the ICON model.

Second: Introducing some new ideas to get that always "final 5%" which can impact one's competitive position, or as importantly one's investment strategy and cash flow prediction.

The detail to which this framework guided our ICON model is extraordinary. Too often things like sales tax, unscheduled product upgrade to sustain a competitive position, and maintenance complexities can take a seemingly profitable situation and turn it into a financial disaster. This framework helped us to integrate all these factors into our ICON model.

SANYA MATHURA

Founder & Managing Director, Strategic Reliability Solutions Ltd, Trinidad and Tobago

Sanya Mathura is a highly accomplished professional in the field of engineering and reliability, with a proven track record of success in providing solutions to complex problems in various industries. She is the Managing Director of Strategic Reliability Solutions Ltd, a leading consulting firm that specializes in helping clients improve their asset reliability and maintenance practices.

Sanya holds a bachelor's degree in electrical and computer engineering as well as a master's in engineering asset management.

As the head of Strategic Reliability Solutions Ltd, Sanya leads a team of highly skilled professionals who provide a wide range of services to clients across various industries, including oil and gas, manufacturing, and transportation. Under her leadership, the company has expanded its services and is now recognized as a leading provider of reliability engineering services in the industry across the globe.

In addition to her work at Strategic Reliability Solutions Ltd, Sanya is an active member of several professional organizations, including the

International Council for Machinery Lubrication (ICML), and writes technical papers for several organizations. She is also a sought-after speaker and has presented at various conferences and seminars on the topics of reliability engineering and lubrication.

She is the first female in the Caribbean to become an ICML-certified MLE (Machinery Lubrication Engineer). Sanya was also the first female in the world to achieve the ICML Varnish badges (VIM & VPR). She is part of the Editorial Board for Precision Lubrication Magazine and writes a lot of technical articles on various platforms.

Sanya also published her first book, "Lubrication Degradation Mechanisms, A Complete Guide," with CRC Press in November 2020. In December 2021 she launched her second book, "Lubrication Degradation – Getting into the Root Causes," co-authored with Bob Latino of Prelical Solutions LLC. Sanya has also co-authored "Machinery Lubrication Technician (MLT) I & II Certification Exam Guide" with Michael Holloway of 5th Order Industry LLC. Recently, she also edited the book, Empowering Women in STEM – Personal Stories and Career Journeys from Around the World.

Sanya's passion for excellence, coupled with her expertise in the field of engineering and reliability, has made her a respected and highly sought-after professional in the industry. Her dedication to providing exceptional service to clients and her commitment to staying up-to-date with the latest industry trends have earned her the respect of her peers and the admiration of her clients.

How do you define Life Cycle Cost Analysis?

Sanya: A LCCA is the determination of the real cost of a product over its useful life from inception to decomposition. Quite often, we may view a product (such as oil being used in a machine) as a defined price, when it is so much more than that. If we think about the life cycle of a lubricant, it actually began millions of years ago when crude oil was developed. Then, there are extraction and refining processes which are involved in developing the base oil to be used for the production of a finished lubricant. Next, there is the research and development, involved in formulating the product, and then the formulation, packaging, and distribution. All of this happens before the user has even seen the product. The product is being used in the equipment; when it reaches its end of life, there is a disposal cost attached to it. My idea of a LCCA is the complete cost of an item from its creation to its disposal, not the end of life as that would have ended when the lubricant could no longer perform its intended functions. It is important to understand the full life cycle of a product before launching into an analysis of its actual cost.

What is the purpose of Life Cycle Cost Analysis?

Sanya: LCCA helps users to truly understand the value that a product can bring to them. In the world of lubrication, users tend to equate the value of the product with the price they paid for it. This is an unfair equation as the product's value is often a lot greater than the price paid for it at the time of purchase. By performing a LCCA, we can easily identify the value that lubricants can bring to the operators and even use this analysis to help justify the use of particular lubricants. For instance, if purchasers move towards a lower-priced product as a method of cost-cutting, a LCCA can demonstrate the actual impact of that lubricant and provide a more accurate method of comparing lubricants.

Your experience of using LCCA?

Sanya: Quite often, when users are selecting lubricants, they tend to focus on the initial price that they have to pay for it from the vendor. We've successfully used LCCA to help demonstrate the true cost of a lubricant and the value that it brings. This final value varies greatly from the initial price.

One example would be the use of synthetic oils vs mineral oils. Typically, synthetic oils are priced at a higher price point compared to mineral oils (in some cases it may be as much as two or five times higher than mineral oils). However, mineral oils typically come to the end of their life within 3–5 years. At this time, they have to be disposed of, the sump of the equipment cleaned, and a new charge of oil bought to replace the previous oil. However, if a synthetic oil is used, this may last for 10–20 years. As such, there would be no disposal cost (every 5 years, which amounts to four disposal costs), there would also be no need to shut down the equipment to have the sump cleaned (4 times over a 20-year period), nor would the purchasers be required to purchase an oil quantity to refill the entire sump during those 20 years. If we're talking about the industrial sector, in particular turbines, these can have very large sumps in excess of 10,000 gallons (37,000 litres) for one turbine. Thus, we have to change the oil in five turbines, that is, 50,000 gallons, which also have to be disposed of and replenished every 5 years. This equates to 200,000 gallons of oil which are disposed of and replenished in a 20-year period. Here LCCA plays a vital role in decision-making by selecting the right lubricant to suit the purpose.

RITU KESARWANI

Consultant and Educator at Zeroing Impact, USA

Ritu Kesarwani lives in Ohio, USA. She has vast experience in consulting and training in diverse streams including Life Cycle Assessment (LCA), circular economy, waste upcycling, and sustainable development. She holds a master's degree in chemical engineering from IIT Bombay, India. Previously, she worked as a Project Developer for a Dutch non-profit organization dedicated to removing plastic from waterways and upcycling it. She served as a chemical process engineer in an engineering and consulting company based in the USA where she was involved in process developments of biodiesel and cellulosic ethanol. She also worked as a deputy manager in a waste management company based in New Delhi, India.

In which type of application, you used LCCA?
Ritu: I mostly used LCCA for educational purposes. I want to implement the knowledge further in industrial applications as well.

Had you used the inflation rate while calculating the Present Value?
Ritu: At the initial stage, I did not incorporate the inflation rate into my calculation of the Present Value. I used only the discount rate. I would like to further expand my knowledge and potentially consider the inflation rate in future analyses.

To what extent do you want to use LCCA methodology in future?
Ritu: I am in the process of learning and applying LCCA to a real project. Though I have not used them extensively so far; however, I am aware of the potential benefits of LCCA methodologies if they are applied suitably as per relevance.

Are you interested in applying LCCA more in your work?
Ritu: Maybe, yes. It will depend on the specific needs and requirements of the future task at hand.

Why do you think that LCCA will be a useful tool?
Ritu: I used to perform Life Cycle Assessment (LCA) for different applications. LCA is a powerful means used to evaluate the environmental impacts of a product, process, or service throughout its entire life cycle.

Doing LCCA while performing LCA has benefits. A separate study again will be tedious. Both LCA and LCCA are valuable frameworks of their own and they both have different outcomes. Improved decision-making may be ensured if the two frameworks align with each other by employing a financial lens to assess the broader social and environmental implications of an investment.

MARCEL SMIT

LCCA Expert, Senior Research Scientist at TNO, Netherlands
Marcel Smit has extensive expertise as a scientist and project manager, mostly in the field of military operations research. Life Cycle Costing (LCC) and Cost Analysis (LCA) are his areas of expertise. Affordability studies, cost-benefit analysis, in-service management, scenario analysis, statistical analysis, operational needs analysis, and logistics are all among his specialities.

Marcel has served in various roles in numerous international working groups linked to cost analysis.

He was the Chairman of the NATO Research and Technology Working Group on "Methods and Models of Life Cycle Costing," and he actively contributed to the preparation of an Allied Publication titled "NATO Guidance on LCC." In addition, he served as the Chairman of an international working group for developing a Code of Practice for LCC analysis. He was also the Chairman of the NATO Missile Defence Project's Cost Analysis Team (CAT).

In 1982, he graduated from Sint Nicolaas Lyceum Amsterdam and completed his Gymnasium. In 1987, he got his postgraduate degree from the University of Amsterdam, with a specialization in Operations Research and Econometrics. He has been a part of the prominent organization TNO since 1989. TNO is an independent applied research organization. It connects people and information to generate solutions that improve industrial competitiveness and societal well-being sustainably.

Marcel has presented many papers at international conferences related to cost analysis. He is also the author of many international journal publications, including "A North Atlantic Treaty Organisation Framework for Life Cycle Costing," which was published in the International Journal of Computer Integrated Manufacturing in 2012. Marcel believes that, as future military acquisition projects become increasingly global, a standard framework is essential to create realistic and consistent LCC estimates for a future system. He created a structure for NATO's cost-cutting procedure. He highlights that LCA is a very important approach for assisting in the most efficient and economical control and management of all necessary and stakeholder multi-criteria needs. As per Marcel, Life Cycle Cost estimate is the single best metric for measuring the value for money, especially in defence programs. LCC estimate can be useful for multiple applications starting from evaluating alternative solutions and source selection to developing future expenditure profiles and evaluating financial risks. As part of the framework, Marcel advises the estimators to define what is to be estimated and understand the purpose of the estimates, prior to initiating LCCA. Also, he emphasizes the clear definition of the assumptions, constraints, and cost breakdown structure to ensure the inclusion of all the relevant cost elements, cost data source and normalization, risk identification, and mitigation for any LCCA.

Marcel has enormous contributions in the field of cost estimation and LCCA for formalizing the procedures, spreading the knowledge, and creating global awareness.

ARIANNA AMATI

Project Management Professional, Italy
Arianna Amati is a Chemical Engineer from Italy who is comfortable performing a wide range of tasks, such as technical, administrative, strategic, and management.

Her background is mainly linked to sustainability, materials, energy transition, and resource efficiency.

In her professional career, she developed skills in the setup and management of projects starting from analysis of eligibility and exclusivity criteria, partner scouting, proposal writing, project coordination, and collection of contributions from partners or colleagues.

Her technical competencies are related to sustainability in detail environmental, social, and economic impact assessments of the novel product, process, and services.

In addition, she acquired competencies in business modelling and planning activities;profitability analysis for new products, exploitation, and intellectual property rights (IPR) issues (e.g., support in the identification of a better strategy for the protection of intellectual property rights); technology scouting; and conceptual design activities. She was involved in various research innovation projects (National and European level) aimed to support the market uptake of new products and services.

For which purpose you used Life Cycle Cost Analysis? How has LCCA helped you in decision-making?

Arianna: In research projects, I had the chance to perform LCCA studies. In the framework of a research project co-funded by the European Commission, I performed different LCCA studies.

The main objective was to compare innovative processes, products, or services with the benchmark solutions. The main advantages were calculating the economic benefit of the new solution, determining a prospective market positioning, identifying the key problem areas, and doing a sensitivity analysis on the OPEX with the greatest impact.

What are the difficulties you faced during Life Cycle Cost Analysis? How did you overcome them?

Arianna: The main difficulties were associated with the cost of some elements. It was difficult to estimate CAPEX for novel equipment or OPEX for the secondary raw material in case of a process that involves recycling. (Secondary raw materials are recycled resources that can be utilized instead of or in addition to virgin raw materials in industrial operations. As a matter of example, the End-of-Life Concrete can be crushed and used as aggregate in the production of fresh concrete.)

I performed LCCA for novel building elements with secondary raw materials. The costs were strongly affected by the secondary raw materials. These costs were associated with different factors such as:

- Processing/recycling process
- Landfill cost
- Business model
- Stakeholders involved in the process.

I performed a sensitivity analysis to mitigate these effects.

SENSITIVITY ANALYSIS

Under a given set of assumptions, sensitivity analysis evaluates how alternative values of an independent variable influence a certain dependent variable. Sensitivity analysis, for instance, may be used to investigate the impact of a rise in inflation of 1% on the present value. What-If scenario might be: "How would the present value change if inflation increased by 1%?" Sensitivity analysis can provide an answer to this question. Sensitivity studies investigate how different sources of uncertainty in a mathematical model contribute to the overall uncertainty of the model.

Do you believe that importance of LCCA will increase in future?
Arianna: Yes, this methodology can cover one very important pillar of sustainability, the economic aspects. Moreover, the LCCA can be very useful in supporting the development of new business models since it can analyze the effect of the involvement of stakeholders.

The LCCA can be used to establish how the costs are affected by the value chain and the business model applied. If you consider different scenarios the costs estimation depends on the value chain and the interaction of the stakeholders involved in the service. For this reason, the LCCA can be used to support business decisions.

You are part of the Iam4Rail flagship project 3. Is Life Cycle Cost Analysis an integral part of the project?
Arianna: Yes, Iam4Rail flagship project 3 is a holistic and integrated Asset Management for Europe's RAIL System which will look into various aspects including minimizing the Life Cycle Costs of assets.

I am part of the project from mid-2023 onwards. So far, my role is concerned, I am involved in the project execution as a facilitator.

> The objective of the FP3 Iam4Rail project is to guarantee comprehensive and integrated asset management for the European rail system's infrastructure and rolling equipment. The goal is to cooperate and comprehensively conduct research, and develop and offer creative solutions, including the establishment of technical standards, requirements, and procedures. In order to satisfy safety goals, and improve the reliability, availability, and capacity of the railway system while minimizing asset life-cycle costs and extending life cycles, the project aims to build on the most cutting-edge technology and concepts.

TASSOS TSOCHATARIDIS, MSC, PMP

Project Management Professional, Civil Engineer, Greece
Tassos Tsochataridis is a certified Project Management Professional from Greece with extensive experience in managing Real Estate Development Projects (residential and commercial). He provides services throughout the life cycle of the investments that include market research, due diligence, financing, design, construction permits and approvals, construction management, facilities management, and sales. He is highly skilled in developing the project schedule, estimating costs, determining the budget, developing and managing the project team, and managing stakeholder engagement.

Tassos is part of the prestigious INTERREG Program "Greece-Bulgaria" as a Project Management Consultant. The main idea behind "INTERREG" is to synergy between neighbouring countries to solve common issues together. Tassos was also a member of the Board of Directors of the Municipal Water and Sewerage Company of Kavala, Greece.

Please share your experience of using LCCA.

Tassos: I am a Project Manager for Real Estate Development Projects. I am basically a civil engineer who did post-graduation in Structural and Environmental Engineering. During my second master's degree in Environmental Engineering, I had my dissertation in LCCA for buildings. During that period, I came across the LCCA methodologies illustrated in this book and found them very useful.

What are the risks associated with LCCA?

Tassos: The risks in LCCA are all about the uncertainty of future costs (and rates such as interest rates). The best way to deal with it at the moment is the Monte Carlo simulation. I used a reputed software for LCCA as an add-on in a standard spreadsheet editor for Risk Analysis, Sensitivity Analysis, and Scenario Analysis.

What is your view on the future of LCCA?

Tassos: I believe LCCA will be the next top thing in the near future, especially in the building sector. I feel that LCCA has not yet explored to its fullest capacity in the building sector across the globe. Also, unfortunately, there is not yet mention of LCCA in highly acclaimed project management professional guidelines. There is a scope to incorporate LCCA formally as an integral part of Project Management.

I hope that the revolution in the field of Artificial Intelligence will be used for LCCA, making it the main method for Investment Evaluation and Decision Making in our sector, as it is the only one that can combine effectively with Life Cycle Assessment (LCA) leading to a more sustainable future for our societies.

Bibliography

Chakravorti, N., 2016. Evaluation of Present Value. *REST Journal on Emerging Trends in Modelling and Manufacturing*, Vol. 2(3), pp. 73–77, ISSN: 2455–4537.

Davis Langdon Management Consulting, 2007. *Life Cycle Costing (LCC) as a Contribution to Sustainable Construction: A Common Methodology*, London: Davis Langdon Management Consulting.

Gillingham, K., 2019. *Carbon Calculus*. [Online] Available at: https://www.imf.org/en /Publications/fandd/issues/2019/12/the-true-cost-of-reducing-greenhouse-gas -emissions-gillingham [Accessed 4 September 2023].

Hoover, K. D., n.d. *Phillips Curve*. [Online] Available at: https://www.econlib.org/library/ Enc/PhillipsCurve.html [Accessed 25 August 2023].

IISD, 2009. *Life Cycle Costing in Sustainable Public Procurement: A Question of Value*, Winnipeg, Manitoba, Canada: International Institute for Sustainable Development (IISD).

Ingemarsdotter, E., n.d. *A Guide to Life Cycle Costing*. [Online] Available at: https:// pre-sustainability.com/articles/life-cycle-costing-in-more-detail/ [Accessed 25 August 2023].

Johnston, K., n.d. *The Disadvantages of Using a Life Cycle Costing Concept*. [Online] Available at: https://smallbusiness.chron.com/disadvantages-using-life-cycle-cost-ing-concept-37919.html [Accessed 31 August 2023].

Perera, O., Morton, B., & Perfrement, T., 2008. *Life Cycle Costing in Sustainable Public Procurement: A Question of Value*, Winnipeg, Canada: International Institute for Sustainable Development.

Planning Planet, 2017. *Managing Cost Estimating & Budgeting - Project Controls*, Craddock, M. (ed.) GCATI.

State of Alaska, Department of Education & Early Development, 1999. *Life Cycle Cost Analysis Handbook*. 1st ed., Juneau, Alaska: State of Alaska, Department of Education & Early Development.

Yosef, S. S., & Kolarik, W. J., 1981. Life Cycle Costing: Concept and Practice. *Omega*, Vol. 9(3), pp. 287–296.

Index

Printed in the United States
by Baker & Taylor Publisher Services